· A COMPLETE GUIDE T

Knitting

· A COMPLETE GUIDE TO ·
Knitting

Pam Dawson

FANFARE BOOKS

Acknowledgements
The diagrams were drawn by
Coral Mula and the pattern pieces by
Colin Salmon.

Photography by Jan Baldwin,
Tom Belshaw, Camera Press,
Steve Campbell, Bill Carter,
Allan Grainger, Chris Harvey,
Clive Helm, Hank Kemme, Di Lewis,
Liz McAulay, Spike Powell,
Tino Tedaldi, Jerry Tubby and
Nick Wright.

Cover design by James Waugh of
Snap Design.
Cover photograph by Leo Lyons.
The publishers would like to thank
Roger King of Gilchrist,
Mandy Perryment and Posh Paws.

This edition published exclusively for
Ferroway Limited (Fanfare Books) in
1985 by Orbis Publishing Limited,
London.

© Eaglemoss Publications Limited,
1983, 1984, 1985.

This material previously appeared in
the partwork *Superstitch*.

ISBN 0-86370-004-7
Printed in Great Britain.

Contents

The knitter's workbox

Knitting is one of the most exciting and rewarding of all the crafts. Every year new and beautiful yarns appear on the market, tools are updated, techniques are modified or rediscovered. This chapter helps you choose the best materials for the job from the wide range available.

Basic knitting techniques have remained virtually unchanged for centuries – some of the earliest known knitted items to survive include Arabian sandal socks dating from the third century BC. In Britain the Elizabethan Age was called 'The Golden Age of Knitting', and the knitters were men.

After the frame knitting machine had been invented, the handcraft was continued in Devon and Cornwall by fishermen, and in the Shetlands by sailors.

Today knitting is more popular than ever before – the only problem is choosing from the wide range of yarns and tools available.

Knitting needles are manufactured in a wide range of sizes in order to achieve various tensions. The greater the figure in millimetres, the larger the diameter of the needles. The most durable needles are made from a pale grey, lightweight, plastic-coated metal for smaller sizes. A lightweight, rigid plastic material is used for the larger sizes. These finishes make for smooth knitting and the needles will not break or chip. Almost any colour of yarn shows up against the uniform grey which makes it easier to count stitches.

Pairs of needles For working to and fro in rows to produce a flat section of knitting, needles are manufactured in pairs. Each needle has a smooth working point at one end and a knob at the other. They can be bought in standard lengths of 25/9, 30/11¾

alpaca

angora

and 35cm/13¾in.

Longer lengths are manufactured but are not so readily available. Large numbers of stitches will need longer needles but personal preference must also be taken into account. Many knitters use long needles so that the left-hand needle can be tucked under the arm to anchor it.

Pairs of colourful plastic needles are also available and children enjoy learning to knit with these. There is a limited range of sizes but they have the advantage of being available in lengths of 15/6, 20/7¾, 25/9¾, 30/11¾ and 35cm/13¾in.

Sets of needles For working in rounds to produce a tubular fabric,

cotton

mohair

camel

cashmere

silk

wool

stitch holder

needles are manufactured in sets of four or five. Each needle is pointed at both ends. They come in the same size range as pairs of needles and in lengths of 20/7¾ and 30cm/11¾in.

Circular needles These can be used for knitting in rounds or in rows. They comprise two pointed needle ends joined together by a thin strip of flexible nylon. They are not made in as many sizes as pairs of needles and are available in lengths of 40/15¾, 60/23½, 80/31½ and 100cm/39½in. It is important to knit with the correct

length of circular needle so that the stitches reach from one needle point to the other.

Other tools Other items in the knitter's workbox include row counters, which fit on to the end of the needle; cable needles – short needles with points at both ends for cabling; stitch holders to keep stitches to be knitted into later while you work the main body of the garment; a needle gauge; a long ruler for measuring sections of knitting; a tape measure for body measurements, a pair of sharp scissors and sewing equipment for joining seams.

Yarn used to mean any natural spun fibre such as wool, cotton or silk, but it now applies to any combination of fibres. The choice is so wide that it is possible to find something to suit all pockets and tastes.

Synthetic yarns are produced by forcing chemical solutions through metal blocks pierced with holes. The size of the holes determines the thickness (denier) of the thread. The extrusion solidifies into long, continuous filaments. Fine filaments are used for tights and stockings. For hand-knitting yarns, thicker filaments are cut into shorter lengths, which are then spun like natural fibres.

All yarns come in standard thicknesses of 2, 3 or 4 ply, double knitting, double double and chunky. The heaviest baby yarn is called quickerknit. Yarns are not spun directly into these thicknesses, but first into plys. **Ply** is the term that describes individual spun threads of fibres. These can be fine or coarse and it is a mistake to think that the ply necessarily indicates the finished thickness of any yarn. A Shetland 2 ply can be just as thick as a normal 4 ply.

A yarn containing 4 plys can be made up of three threads of wool and one of nylon, or any combination of natural and man-made fibres.

Twisting the yarn in a variety of ways forms a workable thread that will not break as it is knitted. Untwisted yarn is very bulky and gives a lot of warmth, but it is difficult for the average knitter to use because it pulls apart easily.

Chemical dyeing is a complex process that produces evenly distributed colour of sufficient depth. Natural dyes rarely achieve this overall consistency of colour.

Dyeing is carried out in batches, or 'lots', of a certain weight. Each time a new batch is required the dye has to be made up again. For this reason, there is often a very slight variation in dye lots. Hand-knitting ball bands give details of the dye lot number as well as the shade number – always make sure that you buy sufficient yarn in the same dye lot, otherwise you might notice the difference when joining in a new ball.

One myth to dispel – there is no such

2 ply   3 ply   4 ply

thing as natural pure white wool! Until the introduction of man-made fibres, the creamy white obtained by bleaching was the accepted standard of whiteness for wool. Man-made fibre treated with fluorescent brightening agents produced brilliant bluewhites but the same dyeing agents used on wool are not always colourfast, and white wool sometimes yellows with age.

Coating processes, such as a shrinkresist finish, are applied to the dyed yarn. One such coating applied to pure wool enables it to be machine washed. Natural wool fibres are like human hair and have tiny saw-like edges. These rub against each other, causing 'felting'. The coating stops the fibres rubbing together.

Weights in which hand-knitting yarn is sold vary from 10 to 100g (grammes). Nearly all yarn is sold by weight rather than length and the amount in each ball may therefore vary slightly.

Once a ball has been wound to give the correct weight, it is secured with a paper ball band. On a branded yarn this will show the spinner's name and the trade name of the yarn; its composition; ply (where applicable); weight; colour and dye lot numbers and, in most instances, codes indicating the correct washing, pressing and dry-cleaning procedures. Always keep a ball band for reference, as it gives valuable information about aftercare.

Substituting needles and yarn may be necessary if you intend to work from a pattern which was published some years ago. A newly published set of knitting instructions will give you the tools and materials that are currently available. To work from an old pattern, use the table overleaf which tells you how to adjust the old British needle sizes to the equivalent metric numbers.

Yarns from natural fibres

Alpaca The hair of the South American llama. A fine, smooth fibre.

Angora The fur of the angora rabbit, found originally in Turkey. An exceptionally soft and fluffy fibre.

Camel hair From the Asiatic camel. A soft, smooth and very warm fibre.

Cashmere The hair of the Himalayan and Tibetan goat. A soft, downy fibre.

Cotton Exceptionally strong fibres obtained from the seed heads of cotton plants, grown mainly in India, Egypt and America.

Mohair The hair of the angora goat, also found originally in Turkey. Long, fluffy fibres.

Silk Delicate fibres obtained from the cocoon of the silkworm, mostly bred in China.

Wool The fleece of the sheep, originally bred in the Middle East. Resilient fibres of varying lengths and qualities.

Yarns from synthetic fibres

Acrylics Fibres such as Courtelle and Orlon, derived from natural gas.
Yarns of high bulk and exceptional lightness. They contain pockets of air, which makes them warm to wear.

Polyamides Fibres such as nylon, produced from chemical sources. These fibres are strong yet elastic. They do not absorb moisture, so are not weakened when wet. Nylon fibres feel a little hard but are excellent strengthening agents when combined with wool or acrylics.

Polyesters Fibres such as Terylene and Crimplene, derived from petrol.
These fibres are strong yet light and do not absorb moisture. On their own, they are subject to static electricity, which attracts dirt, but they combine well with other fibres.

Viscose Regenerated fibres such as rayon obtained from the cellulose in waste cotton and wood pulp. These fibres absorb moisture and are good conductors of heat. They are cool to touch and slippery to

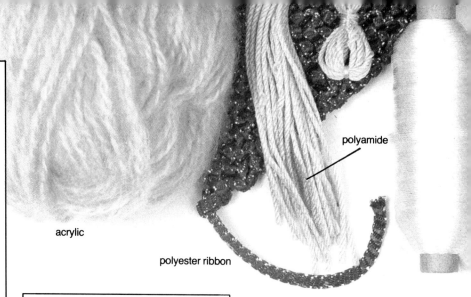

acrylic

polyester ribbon

polyamide

Converting needle sizes

The chart below shows the old Imperial and equivalent metric sizes. A needle gauge giving both sizes will also help you to check old needles, which may not have a size stamped on them.

Imperial	Metric	Imperial	Metric
14	2mm	6	5mm
13	2¼mm	5	5½mm
—	2½mm	4	6mm
12	2¾mm	3	6½mm
11	3mm	2	7mm
10	3¼mm	1	7½mm
—	3½mm	0	8mm
9	3¾mm	00	9mm
8	4mm	000	10mm
7	4½mm		

Converting ounces to grammes

oz balls	25g balls	oz balls	25g balls
1	1	11	13
2	3	12	14
3	4	13	15
4	5	14	16
5	6	15	17
6	7	16	18
7	8	17	19
8	9	18	21
9	10	19	22
10	12	20	23

handle but combine well with other fibres.

Fancy Yarns

Bouclé is a loopy textured yarn. Each ply may be of a different thickness, texture and colour.

Chenille is a velvety, tufted yarn which produces a dense fabric.

Crepe is a very highly-twisted yarn, usually 4 ply or double knitting weights.

chenille

glitter yarns

crepe

viscose ribbon

knop

slub

Glitter yarn is man-made metal threads, used on its own or combined with other fibres.

Slub is an unevenly spun yarn which produces an irregularly textured fabric.

Knop is similar to slub but has small knops in place of thickened streaks.

Abbreviations
A complete list of the abbreviations used in the patterns given in this book can be found on page 28.

bouclé

Casting on and basic stitches

Today's knitting yarns come in a luscious choice of colours and textures. Whether you're an experienced knitter, a bit rusty, or a complete beginner, now is the time to discover how to turn a wealth of traditional stitches into fashionable designs.

Knitting is a straightforward skill that can be picked up in an evening. All you need is a pair of needles, a pattern and some yarn. From there on, learning to knit is like learning to touch-type. It takes a little patience and practice to get the action smooth, with fingers, needles and yarn working in unison. (If you knit jerkily, the knitting will be uneven and bumpy.) There are two basic stitches, knit and purl. They are bread-and-butter stitches, but they combine to produce a vast range of attractive patterns.

Casting on Two methods are given here. Casting on with two needles gives a neat edging and is used with ribbing or stocking stitch. This method is also used when you need to cast on extra stitches further on in the

knitting for buttonholes or to extend the shape. Casting on with one needle gives a ridged edge and so is most suitable for use with garter stitch.

A few helpful hints Hot sticky hands make knitting difficult so always wash your hands. Avoid getting your work dusty by pinning a bag over your work to keep it clean while you knit. Don't stop knitting in the middle of a row, but always continue to the end. Remember not to stick the needles into the ball of yarn as this can split the yarn. When you start to knit a piece which has been left for some weeks, it is a good idea to unpick the last row worked before continuing to knit. This overcomes any distortion of stitches by the needles and eliminates uneven fabric.

How to hold the yarn and needles

1

2

1 The needle in your right hand is used to make the stitches, while the needle in your left hand holds the completed stitches.
2 Wind the yarn round the fingers of

your right hand so that it flows smoothly and freely over your fingers. This helps you to knit evenly. The main thing is to feel comfortable and relaxed.

Casting on
with two needles

Knitting begins with a slip loop
which counts as the first stitch. To
make a loop take the main length of
yarn across the short end.
1 Using the point of a needle, pull the
main length through from the back to
the front and leave this loop on the
needle.
Draw up the main length to tighten
the loop.

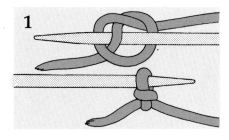

2 Hold the needle with the slip
loop in your left hand and the free
needle in your right hand,
carrying the main length of yarn
across your right hand.

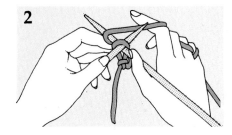

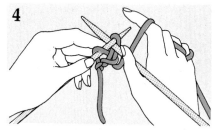

3 Insert the point of the right-hand
needle into the slip loop from the
front to the back, take the yarn
under and round the point.

Draw the yarn through the slip loop
to make a stitch. Put the new stitch
on to the left-hand needle without
twisting it.

4 *To make the next stitch insert the
needle from the front to the back but
this time *between* the two stitches.
Take the yarn (as before) under and
round the point and draw the yarn

through on to the right-hand needle
to make another stitch. Put the new
stitch on the left-hand needle
without twisting it.

Continue in this way from the point
marked with an asterisk (*) until you
have cast on the required number of
stitches.

Casting on with one needle

This method uses only one needle because the thumb of the left hand replaces the other needle – so it is sometimes called the thumb method. Begin by making a slip loop about 50cm/20in from end of a ball of yarn. This should be enough yarn to make about 25 stitches in double knitting yarn with 4mm/No 8 needles – leave a longer end if you are going to need more stitches.

1 Hold the needle with the slip loop in your right hand and wind the main length of yarn round the fingers of your right hand. With the fingers of your left hand hold the end of yarn as shown.

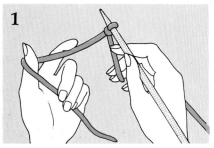

2 *Insert the needle through the loop round your thumb.

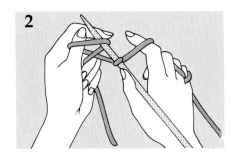

3 Take the main length of yarn under and over the point with your right hand and draw the yarn through on to the needle to make a stitch.

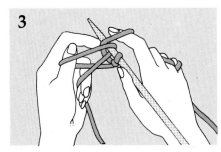

4 Leave this stitch on the needle and tighten the end of yarn. Wind the

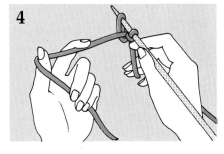

end of yarn round your thumb again, ready to make the next stitch.

Continue in this way from the point marked with an asterisk (*) until you have cast on the required number of stitches.

To knit stitches

Hold the needle with the cast-on stitches in your left hand and the free needle and yarn in your right hand.

1 Insert the right-hand needle from the front to the back into the front loop of the first stitch of the row. *Holding the yarn at the back of the work throughout the row, take it under and round the point.

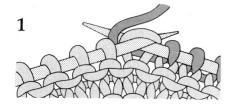

2 Draw the yarn through on to the right-hand needle.

3 Leave this new stitch on the right-hand needle and allow the old stitch to drop off the left-hand needle. One stitch has been knitted and is abbreviated as K1. Insert the right-hand needle from the front to the back into the front loop of the

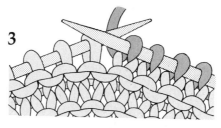

next stitch. Continue from the point marked with an asterisk (*) until all the cast-on stitches have been knitted on to the right-hand needle. At the end of this row transfer the needle holding the stitches to your left hand, with the yarn again at the right-hand end of the row, ready to start the next row of knitting.

To purl stitches

Hold the needle with the cast-on stitches in your left hand and the free needle and yarn in your right hand.

1 Insert the right-hand needle from right to left into the front loop of the first stitch of the row. *Holding the yarn at the front of the work throughout the row, take it over the top and round the point.

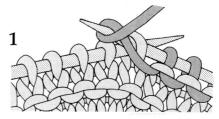

2 Draw the yarn through on to the right-hand needle.

3 Leave this new stitch on the right-hand needle and allow the old stitch to drop off the left-hand needle. One stitch has been purled and is abbreviated as P1. Insert the right-hand needle from right to left into the front loop of the next stitch.

3

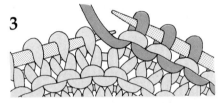

Continue from the point marked with an asterisk (*) until all the cast-on stitches have been purled on to the right-hand needle.
Transfer the needle holding the stitches to your left hand, with the yarn again at the right-hand end of the row, ready to start the next row.

To knit and purl in the same row

You can build up interesting reversible patterns by knitting and

1

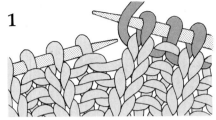

purling in the same row. When changing from a knit to a purl stitch remember to hold the yarn in the correct position. Bring it forward

2

between the needles to purl and take it back between the needles to knit. If you don't, the yarn will be carried across the right-hand needle and you will find you have created an extra stitch.

Stocking stitch

When the first and every following odd-numbered row is knitted and the second and every following even row is purled, it produces stocking stitch.
The right (knitted) side of this pattern is the smoothest of all knitted fabrics. The wrong (purled) side is called reversed stocking stitch. It does not look the same on both sides.

Garter stitch

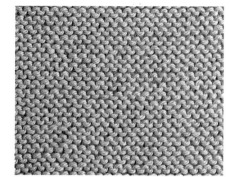

(The three stitches shown here are all reversible, which means they look the same on both sides.)

When each stitch in every row is knitted, this is called garter stitch. The effect is a horizontal, ridged pattern.
It can be made quickly and without too much concentration so it is ideal for a beginner. Unlike stocking stitch, a slight unevenness of stitch is acceptable.

Single ribbing

Working single knit and purl stitches alternately across a row – K1, P1, K1, P1 – produces single ribbing, which is reversible. Remember to bring the yarn into the correct position when changing between knitting and purling.
All the stitches which were *knitted* in the previous row must be *purled* and all the purled stitches must be knitted.
It holds its shape very well and is used for cuffs and neckbands.

Basket stitch

This reversible pattern needs a number of stitches cast on which will divide by six, eg 30.
1st row *Knit 3 stitches, called K3, purl 3 stitches, called P3, continue from the * to the end.
Repeat this row 3 times more.
5th row *P3 stitches, K3 stitches, continue from the * to the end.
Repeat the 5th row 3 times more.
These 8 rows form the pattern, which resembles woven basketwork.

Casting off and simple seams

Casting off is an art in itself. Discover the different techniques used for casting off on a knitted, purled, or ribbed row and a really original way to deal with that ugly last loop which even experienced knitters sometimes get at the end of the cast off row. Knowing how to join new yarn and seam sections together properly gives your knitting a professional finish.

Casting off is the method used for finishing off a completed section of knitting or for certain types of shaping such as armholes or shoulders.

When you are ready to cast off, continue to knit or purl the stitches in the cast-off row as the pattern dictates. If the stitches are not cast off in the correct pattern sequence, you will spoil the appearance of the work and make seaming more difficult.

Aim to keep the cast off stitches regular and even, otherwise this edge may pull the whole garment out of shape. Some instructions emphasize that stitches must be cast off loosely, for example at a neck edge where the fabric needs to be flexible. If you find you cast off too tightly, use one size larger needle in your right hand to work the stitches, before casting off.

Three ways of casting off

Casting off on a knitted row

Knit the first two stitches in the usual way and leave them on the right-hand needle.
1 *Insert the left-hand needle into the first of the stitches worked on to the

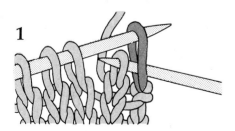

1

right-hand needle. Lift this over the top of the second stitch and off the needle. One stitch has been cast off and one stitch remains on the right-hand needle.
2 Knit the next stitch and leave this on the right-hand needle. Continue from the point marked with an

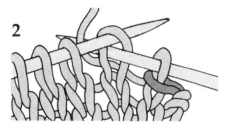

2

asterisk (*), until all the stitches have been cast off and one stitch remains on the right-hand needle.
Fasten off this last stitch by breaking yarn, leaving an end 10cm/ 4in long. Draw this end through the last stitch and pull it up tightly.

Casting off on a purled row

Work this in exactly the same way as for casting off on a knitted row, but purl each stitch instead of knitting it, before casting it off.

Casting off on a ribbed row

Rib the first two stitches and leave them on the right-hand needle.
*Insert the left-hand needle into the first stitch worked on the right-hand needle. Lift this over the top of the second stitch and off the needle.

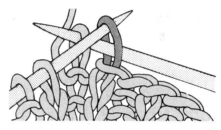

Rib the next stitch and leave this on the right-hand needle. Continue from the point marked with an asterisk (*), until all the stitches have been cast off and one stitch remains on the right-hand needle. Fasten off this last stitch.

Seaming

For successful results in knitting you need to pay as much attention when sewing sections together as when knitting them.

The four sections of the mohair T-top on page 24 are sewn together using a flat seam, one of the two simple and effective methods given below. Always tack the pieces together first as this will help you to ensure that you match stitches and row ends. This is important when knitting stripes.

Simple flat seaming

Flat seaming is suitable when you have been knitting with thick yarn. (Use a finer yarn of the same shade if you are sewing up mohair because it is almost impossible to sew with.) Use a blunt-ended sewing needle with a large eye.
Put the right sides of both sections of knitting together and sew from right to left.
Secure the yarn at the beginning of the seam with a few running stitches. Place the first finger of your left hand between the sections.
*Sewing one stitch in from the edge, push the needle through from the back section across to the corresponding stitch on the front section. Pull the yarn through.
Move along the width of one row. Push the needle through the front section to the corresponding stitch on the back section. Pull the yarn through.
Continue in this way from the asterisk (*), along the seam.
Finish off with running stitches to secure the yarn.

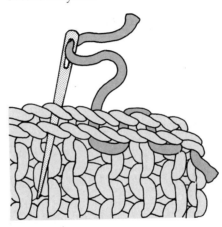

Simple oversewn seam

This method can be used to join stitches to row ends or along any edge where the minimum of bulk is required. It should also be used to join ribbing and fine fabrics. It draws the edges together very neatly, but take care not to pull the sewing yarn up too tightly as it will form a tight ridge.
As with flat seaming, use a blunt-ended needle with a large eye. Place the two edges together with the right sides facing each other. Secure the yarn at the beginning of the seam with a few running stitches.
*Take the needle over the top of the edges and through one loop at the edge on both pieces. Pull the yarn through.
Continue in this way from the point marked with an asterisk (*), along the seam to give a lacing effect. Keep the stitches even and do not draw them up too tightly. Finish off with a few running stitches to secure the yarn.

Start with a mohair scarf

A mohair scarf is a welcome luxury in cold weather – better still, its fluffiness conceals the uneven fabric that some beginners may produce. The design uses two reversible stitches shown on page 17. If you wish, the scarf can be worked entirely in garter stitch, single rib or basket stitch. It measures about 18cm×142cm/7in×56in.

You will need

5×25g balls of Jaeger Mohair Spun, plain or with glitter
One pair 5½mm/No 5 needles

Scarf

Cast on 30 stitches by the one-needle method.
Work 10 rows garter stitch.
Work 16 rows basket stitch. 26 rows in all.
Repeat these 26 rows 11 times more.
Work 10 rows garter stitch.

Two new methods of seaming

Back stitch seam

Place the right sides of the pieces together. Work along the wrong side of the fabric from right to left, one stitch in from the edge. Secure the yarn at the beginning of the seam with two or three small stitches, one on top of the other.

1 *With the sewing needle at the back of the fabric, move along to the left the width of one knitted stitch from the last stitch and push the

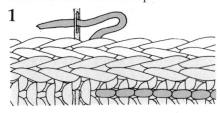

1

needle through both pieces to the front at right-angles to the edge. Pull the yarn through.

2 Take the needle across the front of the fabric from left to right and push it through both pieces at the end of the last sewing stitch to the back. Pull the yarn through.

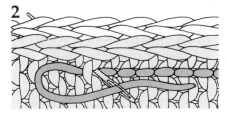

Continue from the * until the seam is completed. Fasten off with two or three small stitches.

Invisible seam

With the *right side* of both pieces facing you, lay them one above the other. The seam can be joined from right to left or left to right. Secure the yarn with two or three small stitches one on top of the other on the lower piece. Pass the needle across to the first stitch on the upper piece, pick up the bar between the first and second stitch in from the edge and pull the yarn through.

1 *Pass the needle across to the stitch on the same row on the lower piece, pick up the bar between the first and second stitch in from the edge and pull the yarn through.

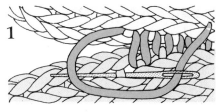

2 Pass the needle across to the next stitch on the next row on the upper piece, pick up the bar between the first and second stitch in from the edge and pull the yarn through. Continue from the * until the seam is completed, pulling each stitch up to the same tension as the fabric. Fasten off with two or three small stitches.

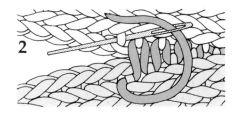

A neat method of hemming

Slip stitch hemming

Turn in the hem or facing and have the wrong side of the main fabric facing you. Secure the yarn to the hem or facing with two or three small stitches on top of each other.
1 *Insert the needle from right to left and lightly pick up *one thread only* of a stitch to the left on the main

1

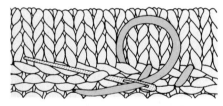

fabric. Pull the yarn through fairly loosely.
2 Move along the fabric to the left, insert the needle into the hem or facing and lightly pick up *one thread only* of a stitch. Pull yarn through. Continue from the * until the hem is completed. Fasten off with two or three small stitches.

2

Joining in a new ball of yarn

Whether you are knitting with just one colour of yarn or using stripes of different colours, you must always join in a new ball at the beginning of a row, never in the middle. This means you have to judge how much yarn you need to work the last row of the ball. Usually, a piece of yarn about four times the width of the knitting is enough to knit a row.

Joining with a reef knot

Where the same colour is being knitted throughout, join the new ball to the finished one with a reef knot. Take the end of the old ball of yarn from left to right over and under the end of the new ball. Take the same end from right to left over and under the other end, to form a loose reef knot.

When this piece of knitting has been completed, tighten up the reef knot. Darn in the ends along the edge of the fabric, before beginning to seam.

Joining with a slip loop

Where coloured stripes are being

reef knot

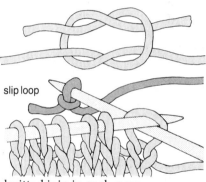

slip loop

knitted join in each new colour with a slip loop. The first stitch will then be in the new colour. Break off the old colour, leaving an end to be darned in along the back of the last row in this colour. Form the end of the new ball into a slip loop. Insert the right-hand needle into the front of the first stitch of the row. Put the slip loop on to the right-hand needle and pull this loop through to complete the stitch in the usual way. Continue knitting with the new colour.

Dropped stitch

This is not easy for a beginner to put right as it must be picked up and worked in according to the pattern. Therefore take care to check the number of stitches at the end of every row. This may seem time-consuming, but it is easier than discovering you have dropped a stitch several rows back. As an emergency measure if you have been unlucky enough to drop a stitch in the row you have

just worked, secure it with a small safety pin. This will stop it unravelling.

On the next row, when you reach the dropped stitch put it back on to the left-hand needle and continue. This may leave an unworked thread, but is not as unsightly as a ladder.

T-shaped mohair jersey

Often the most effective designs are the simplest. If you are working with a dramatically beautiful and textured yarn such as mohair, you want to choose stitches and shapes that let the yarn speak for itself, rather than compete. It is a bonus that the fluffy mohair will disguise uneven knitting. This T-shaped jersey is knitted in four pieces – two identical pieces for the front and the back, and two identical pieces which combine yoke and sleeves. In this simple pattern none of the pieces needs shaping.

It can be knitted in three colours, as photographed right, or all in the same colour. (If you knit it all in one colour you will need 15 balls of yarn.)

Sizes

The jersey will fit a medium bust size, 86–91cm/34–36in, loosely Length to shoulder, 57cm/22½in

You will need

7×25g balls of plain Jaeger Mohair Spun (67% mohair, 28% wool, 5% nylon) in colour A
5×25g balls of Jaeger Mohair Spun with glitter in colour B
3×25g balls of plain Jaeger Mohair Spun in colour C
One pair 5½mm/No 5 needles

Back and front

With plain yarn in colour A cast on 78 stitches by the one-needle method. This is the bottom of the jersey and should measure 48cm/19in across after you have knitted about 5cm/2in. If it is more than this you are knitting too loosely. Unravel this piece of knitting and start again with 5mm/No 6 needles. If it is less, you are knitting too tightly and should change to 6mm/No 4 needles.
Work 10 rows garter stitch. Break off yarn. Join in glitter yarn in colour B with a slip loop.
Work 16 rows basket stitch. Break off yarn. Join in plain yarn in colour A with a slip loop.
Work 10 rows garter stitch. Break off yarn. Join in plain yarn in colour C with a slip loop.
Work 14 rows stocking stitch. Break off plain yarn in colour C. Join in yarn in colour A with a slip loop. 50 rows

have been worked.
Repeat the first 36 rows once more.
Cast off.
Make another piece in same way.

Yoke and sleeve section

With plain yarn in colour A cast on
36 stitches as given for body.
Repeat 50 pattern rows as given for
body 4 times in all, then first 36 rows
once more. Cast off.
Make another piece in same way.

To make up

Do not press, as this will flatten
garter and basket stitch. Darn in all
ends – see joining with a slip loop.
Check the rows of stocking stitch to
see which is the right side.
With right sides of yoke together and
edges without any yarn changes (see
diagram), join top arm and shoulder
with flat seams, leaving 27cm/10¾in
open in centre for neck. Turn in a
few stitches at neck edge and lightly
stitch down to neaten.
Mark centre of yoke and centre of
body pieces with a contrasting
coloured thread. Join cast off edge of
body pieces to centre of yoke and
sleeve sections. Join side and sleeve
seams.

How to read knitting patterns

The key to successful knitting lies in following the pattern exactly – and this means knowing how to read and carry out the instructions.

Before you begin to knit – even before you buy the yarn – always make sure to read your pattern thoroughly from beginning to end.

The designer works out tension, yarn thickness and needle size to suit the style of the garment and the pattern of the fabric, and these must be followed exactly for good results. Pay particular attention to the making-up section – even a simple shape may require intricate seaming or trimming.

Pattern writers use abbreviations and symbols in knitting instructions to save space. If in doubt, refer to the list of abbreviations given on page 28 at the end of this book.

Patterns give instructions in full for a specific stitch or technique the first time it is used, followed by its abbreviated form. From then on, only the abbreviation is given.

Symbols also denote working methods. A single asterisk, *, means that the instructions that follow it must be repeated to the end of the row, or until a given number of stitches remains at the end of the row. Further instructions for working these remaining stitches will be given to complete the row.

An asterisk can also indicate that instructions will be repeated at a later stage in the knitting. When knitting a jersey, the pattern for back and front may well be the same to a certain point. A double asterisk, **, signals the end of the repeat.

Any instructions in round brackets, (), apply to all sizes. Instructions shown in square brackets [], denote larger sizes.

The instructions in knitting patterns are divided under a series of headings.

Sizes

This heading gives the finished measurements of the garment, the smallest size first, the larger sizes following in order in square brackets []. Some designs are given only in small sizes because they would not flatter a more generous figure. Some patterned designs are given only in one size because the pattern repeats are so large that one more or less would not give a standard size.

If you underline the figures that apply to your size you will be able to pick them out more quickly as you knit.

You will need

This heading lists the type and brand name of the yarn needed; the needle sizes and any additional tools such as cable needles; and trimmings, such as buttons. Make sure you have everything to hand before beginning to knit.

Tension

This heading gives the key to perfect knitting. Check your tension very carefully, especially if you are using a substitute yarn.

Note

This heading draws your attention to any unusual aspect of the pattern, such as the use of separate balls of yarn to work a coloured pattern.

Making up

This section tells you how to assemble the pieces you have knitted and add any finishing touches. Pay as much attention to these instructions as you did to the rest of the pattern for a really professional finish. Check with the ball band whether you should press the yarn, particularly if you have used a substitute. Sew the pieces together in the order given in the instructions – you may have to add edgings and trimmings before seaming. Never skimp on trimmings – it is better to buy a little too much ribbon than to find yourself short.

Pattern problems

Fortunately there are ways of rectifying your mistakes if you should happen to misread a knitting pattern. If you have misread a pattern row, throwing the following rows out of sequence, follow the instructions below to unpick the stitches – only pull your knitting off the needles as a last resort! If you drop a stitch and it has unravelled for a number of rows it will spoil the look of your knitting. You can use a crochet hook to pick it up.

1 To unpick stitches on a knit row

Insert the left-hand needle from the front to the back into the stitch *below* the first stitch on the right-hand needle. Remove the right-hand needle and pull the yarn to unravel the stitch. Keep the yarn at the *back* of the work and repeat this process until the required number of stitches have been unpicked.

2 To unpick stitches on a purl row

Insert the left-hand needle from the front to the back into the stitch *below* the first stitch on the right-hand needle. Remove the right-hand needle and pull the yarn to unravel the stitch. Keep the yarn at the *front* of the work and repeat this process until the required number of stitches have been unpicked.

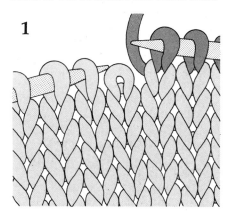

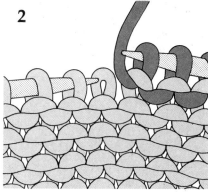

3 To pick up a dropped stitch on knitted side of stocking stitch

Insert a crochet hook from front to back through the dropped stitch. Put the hook under the thread lying between the stitches on each side of the dropped stitch. Pull this thread through the dropped stitch and leave it on the hook. Repeat this process until the dropped stitch is level with the last row worked. Put the loop on to the left-hand needle and knit it.

If the last row being worked is a purl row, turn the work to the purl side and purl the loop.

3

4 To pick up a dropped purl stitch in a patterned row

Insert the crochet hook from back to front through the dropped stitch. *Put the hook over the thread lying between the stitches on each side of the dropped stitch and pull this

4

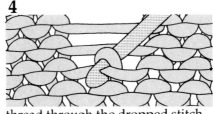

thread through the dropped stitch. Slip the loop on to a cable needle and remove the hook. Insert the

hook into the loop again and continue from * until the dropped stitch is level with the last row worked. Put the loop on to the left-hand needle and purl it.

To pick up a dropped stitch in garter stitch

Alternate the knit and purl methods to keep the ridged sequence correct.

Knitting pattern abbreviations

alt	alternate(ly)
approx	approximate(ly)
beg	begin(ning)
ch	chain(s)
cm	centimetre(s)
cont	continu(e)(ing)
cr2L	cross 1 knit st to left
cr2R	cross 1 knit st to right
dec	decreas(e)(ing)
foll	follow(ing)
g st	garter stitch
g	gramme(s)
inc	increas(e)(ing) by working twice into a stitch
K	knit
K up	pick up and knit, as round neck edge
K-wise	knitwise direction
m	metre(s)
MB	make bobble, as specified
mm	millimetre(s)
M1	make one by picking up loop lying between needles and knit through back of loop to increase one
patt	pattern
psso	pass slipped stitch over
p2sso	pass 2 slipped stitches over
P	purl
P up	pick up and purl
P-wise	purlwise direction
rem	remain(ing)
rep	repeat(ing)

Rs	right side of fabric
sl	slip
sl st	slip stitch(es)
st(s)	stitch(es)
st st	stocking stitch
tog	together
tw2B	twist 2 knit stitches to left
tw2F	twist 2 knit stitches to right
tw2PB	twist 2 purl stitches to left
tw2PF	twist 2 purl stitches to right
Ws	wrong side of fabric
ybk	yarn back between needles
yfwd	yarn forward between needles
yon	yarn over needle
yrn	yarn around needle

Pattern symbols

An asterisk, *, in a pattern row denotes that the stitches after this sign must be repeated from that point to the end of the row, or to the last number of stitches given. Instructions shown in round brackets (), denote that this section of the pattern is to be worked for all sizes. Instructions shown in square brackets, [], denote larger sizes.

How to increase

Adding five ways of increasing to your basic technique widens your knitting horizons considerably. Each of the methods described here has a different purpose. One method, decorative increasing, is used in the pattern for making a shawl for a baby or for yourself.

Whether a jersey fits well or not depends on the basic concept behind its design, and one of the most critical aspects of design is the shaping. Knitting patterns usually indicate when shaping is about to begin but do not always give details of the exact method to use. Knowing which is the best method for the job is the mark of a professional.

To increase means to add or make stitches and there are various ways of increasing the width and varying the shape of knitting. Single stitches added at regular intervals to the ends of the rows gradually change the shape of the knitting, such as when shaping a sleeve. Stitches added at intervals across the row change the shape of the knitting from within,

creating panels such as those often found on matinée jackets. Large numbers of stitches added on at the ends of rows alter the outline of the knitting immediately, as with sleeves worked all in one with the body.

This chapter gives you three methods for increasing gradually and one for adding multiples of extra stitches and it gives you the necessary information to select the best method for you.

Working twice into a stitch is the simplest way of increasing and it is used to make an extra stitch at each end of the same row, as in sleeve shaping. It is abbreviated as inc 1 (increase one).

The extra stitch always appears after the stitch it is worked into, making a little 'pip' in the fabric. It is ideal for

use in garter stitch where the pip will not show. Do not use it in stocking stitch, particularly in the middle of a row, as it affects the smooth texture of the knitting. Never use this method to increase more than one stitch at a time.

Increasing between stitches is the method used for increasing in the middle of a row. It does not spoil the appearance of the fabric and so is the best method for increasing patterned stitches where the pip increase would spoil the sequence of the pattern. It is also suitable for stocking stitch and can be used to increase at the ends of each row. It is abbreviated as M1 (make one).

This method is particularly useful for picking up stitches on either side of a central stitch, as on v-neck shaping.

Decorative increasing (also known as eyelet hole increasing) is another method for increasing at any point in a row.

It forms an eyelet hole in the fabric and is abbreviated in various ways (see Decorative increasing, page 33), depending on whether you are knitting or purling and forms the basis of most lace patterns. This method involves putting the yarn over or round the needle which makes an extra stitch without knitting one.

Invisible increasing is a useful method of increasing, so called because it is hard to detect. It is used on stocking stitch because it is the only method which does not spoil the appearance of this stitch. It can be used at each end of a row, inside the edge stitches or in the middle of a row and so is very versatile.

This method is particularly useful for increasing three or four consecutive stitches in a row because if you keep the extra stitches fairly loose it does not affect the tension.

Multiples of extra stitches sometimes need to be added to a section of knitting, in which case extra stitches must be cast on. This can be done at the beginning and end of a row, or to replace stitches which have been cast off in a previous row, as for a buttonhole.

Working twice into the same stitch

Note: When increasing at the end of a row, work the increase one stitch earlier to ensure that the position of the pip is the same on the right edge as on the left. (Because the extra stitch is formed one in from the edge seaming is easier.)

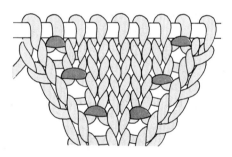

To increase a knitted stitch at the beginning of a row

Work the first stitch but do not drop it off the left-hand needle. Insert the right-hand needle into the *back* loop of the same stitch and knit it again, then drop the stitch off the left-hand needle.

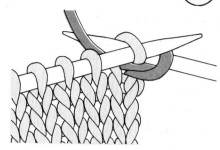

To increase a knitted stitch at the end of a row

Work until two stitches remain on the left-hand needle. Knit twice into the next stitch as at the beginning of a row, then knit the last stitch.

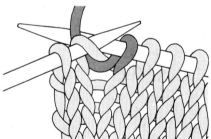

To increase a purled stitch at the beginning of a row

1 Work the first stitch but do not drop it off the left-hand needle.

Insert the right-hand needle from left to right through the *back* loop of the same stitch and purl it again, then drop the stitch off the left-hand needle.

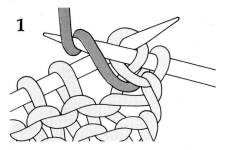

2 Purling twice into the front is not so satisfactory because it forms two loops round the right-hand needle. On the next row you must work into the front of the first loop and into the back of the second loop.

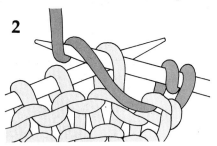

To increase a purled stitch at the end of a row

Work until two stitches remain on the left-hand needle. Purl twice into the next stitch as at the beginning of a row, then purl the last stitch.

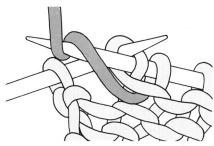

Increasing between stitches

Note: If you work three stitches (for example) and increase one and on

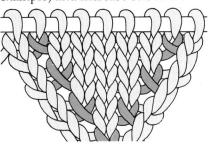

the next increasing row you work three stitches and increase one, the increase slants to the right. If you work an extra stitch each time before increasing, it slants to the left.

To make one in a knitted row

1 Work until the position for the increase is reached. Use the right-hand needle to pick up the thread lying between the stitch just worked and the next stitch on the left-hand needle. Put this loop or the left-hand needle.

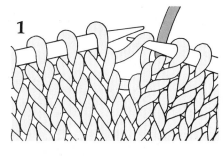

2 Knit into the *back* of the loop, this twists the stitch and avoids a hole in the fabric. (Knitting into the front leaves an open space beneath the increased stitch.)

2

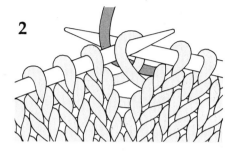

To make one in a purled row

1 Work until the position for the increase is reached. Use the right-hand needle to pick up the thread lying between the stitch just worked and the next stitch on the left-hand needle. Put this loop on the left-hand needle.

1

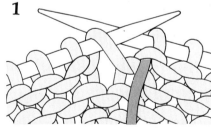

2 Purl into the back of it by inserting the right-hand needle from left to right into the back loop to twist the stitch. (Purling into the front leaves an open space beneath the increased stitch.)

2

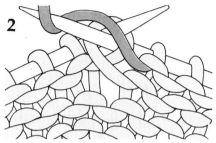

Decorative increasing (eyelet hole)

To make a stitch between two knitted stitches

Bring the yarn forward between the two needles. Take the yarn over the top of the right-hand needle ready to knit the next stitch. This is abbreviated as 'yfwd'.

To make a stitch between a purled and a knitted stitch

Carry the yarn, which is already at the front of the work, over the top of the right-hand needle ready to knit the next stitch. This is abbreviated as 'yon'.

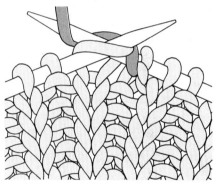

To make a stitch between two purled stitches

Take the yarn over the top of the right-hand needle. Bring it forward between the two needles to the front again ready to purl the next stitch. This is abbreviated as 'yrn'.

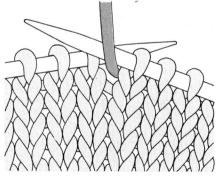

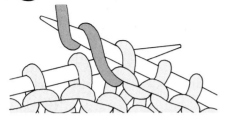

To make a stitch between a knitted and a purled stitch

Bring the yarn forward between the two needles. Carry it over the top of the right-hand needle, then between the two needles to the front again ready to purl the next stitch. This is also abbreviated as 'yrn'.

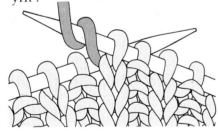

Adding multiples of extra stitches

To add at the beginning of a row

Cast on the number of stitches required at the beginning of a row by the two-needle method (page 13). Work across these stitches then continue along the row. (The easiest way to add stitches at each end is to cast on at the beginning of two consecutive rows.)

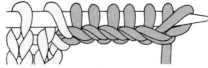

To add at the end of a row

After working across a row, cast on the number of stitches required by the one-needle method (page 14). With a separate length of the same yarn make a slip loop on the left-hand needle. Work into this

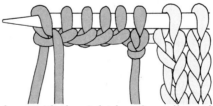

loop with the right-hand needle and the main length of yarn. Wind the short end round the thumb and use the main length to cast on the number of stitches required.

Soft looped shawl

Simple garter stitch is used for this soft, light shawl. Use white for a baby or try a bright colour for yourself. Winding the yarn round the needle at the beginning of the row forms an eyelet increase. Use this as a decorative edging on its own or thread a coloured ribbon through for a splash of colour.

Size

Width across top edge 155cm/62in
Depth from top edge to centre point 82cm/32¼in.

You will need

9×20g balls of Patons Fairy Tale Double Knitting
One pair of 6½mm/No 3 needles
4m/4¼yd of 1cm/½in-wide ribbon

Tension

16 sts and 26 rows to 10cm/4in over garter st worked on 6½mm/No 3 needles.

Shawl

Beg at lower edge, with 6½mm/No 3 needles cast on 2 sts. K one row.
Next row Loop yarn round right-hand needle to inc 1, K to end. 3 sts.

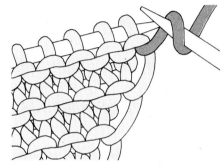

Next row Inc 1, K to end including loop on needle. 4 sts.
Rep the last row until there are 200 sts.
Cast off loosely.

To make up

Do not press. Cut ribbon into two 2m/2⅛yd lengths. Thread through side loops along edges and tie in a bow at centre point at beginning of work. Loop ribbon into bows at top corners and stitch to hold.

How to decrease

Knowing how to reduce the overall width of knitted fabric is an essential part of basic techniques. Five ways are described here and each has a different purpose. Practise all these methods so that you can use the correct shaping in your knitting patterns.

Decreasing the number of stitches in the width of a piece of knitting alters its size and shape. Knitting patterns usually indicate when shaping is about to begin but do not always give details of the exact method to use. Each one has a different appearance and purpose and this chapter shows you how to choose the best method for your particular pattern. The samples are worked in stocking stitch so that you can see the angle of decrease clearly, but the methods are the same for other stitch combinations.

Depending on which method you use, the decreased stitches slant either to the right or to the left. As a general rule, the slant should follow the line of the knitting. So when decreasing at the beginning of a row, the stitches should slant inwards to the left and at the end of a row they should slant inwards to the right. To work decreases in pairs, one at each end of a row, the decrease at the beginning of the row slants to the left and at the end, it slants to the right. This rule need not apply when the shaping serves a decorative purpose – for example when it highlights the fully-fashioned seams on a raglan-sleeved jersey. Here the decreased stitches are meant to show up and look most effective when worked against the line of the knitting – those at the beginning of the row slanting outwards to the right and those at the end of the row outwards to the left.

Working stitches together is the simplest way to decrease one or two knitted or purled stitches at any given point in a row. Use it when decreasing at the beginning of a purled row and at the end of a knitted row, but don't work the first or the last stitch together with its neighbour or you will create an uneven edge, difficult for seaming. When stitches are worked together in this way, the decreased stitches all slant to the *right* on the knitted side of stocking stitch.

Decreasing in a vertical line, as for a gored skirt, is achieved by using both angles of decreasing. Working across the first decreasing row all the decreased stitches should slant to the *right*. Working across the next decreasing row they should all slant to the *left*. By continuing to alternate the angle a vertical line is formed.

Working stitches together through the back of the loops is a method which results in the decreased stitches slanting to the *left* on the knitted side of stocking stitch. So use this method when decreasing at the beginning of a knitted row and at the end of a purled row. However, the slip and knit or purl stitch method (detailed below) is simpler and more commonly used.

Slip and stitch decreasing is the simplest method to use at the beginning of a knitted row, using the knit two together method at the end of the same row so that the decreases form pairs, one slanting to the left and one to the right. The slip and knit stitch method results in the decreased stitch slanting to the *left* on the knitted side of stocking stitch.

Slip and purl stitch decreasing creates decreased stitches slanting to the *right* on the knitted side of stocking stitch but is less commonly used than purling stitches together.

Casting off multiples of stitches. Use this method if you need to subtract more than one or two stitches from a section of knitting. This can be done at the beginning or the end of a row, as for the underarms of a jersey. When shaping a neck, a group of stitches is cast off in the centre of a row. Stitches also need to be cast off for details such as buttonholes.

Working stitches together

To decrease one knitted stitch at the beginning of a row
Knit the first stitch. Insert the right hand needle through the next two stitches as if to knit them. Knit them

both together and drop them off the left-hand needle. The abbreviation for this is 'K2 tog'.

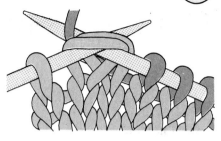

To decrease two knitted stitches at the beginning of a row
Knit three stitches together instead of two. The abbreviation for this is 'K3 tog'.

To decrease one or two stitches in the middle of a row, work until the position for the decrease is reached. Knit the next stitches together as for the beginning of a row.

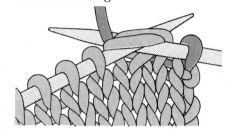

To decrease one or two knitted stitches at the end of a row
Work until three or four stitches remain on the left-hand needle. Knit the next two or three stitches together as for the beginning of a row and knit the last stitch.

To decrease one or two purled stitches
The methods are the same as for knitting stitches together but the stitches are purled together. Decreasing one stitch is abbreviated as 'P2 tog' and decreasing two stitches as 'P3 tog'.

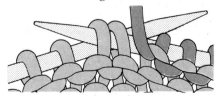

Decreasing in a vertical line

To decrease two stitches in a vertical line

1 Slip one stitch, knit or purl the next two stitches together, (purling through the back of the loops).

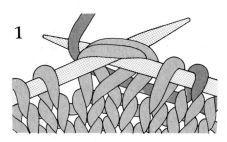

2 Lift the slipped stitch over and off the right-hand needle. The slipped stitch and the two stitches worked

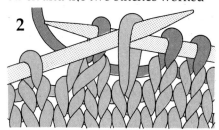

together slant in towards each other. The knitted version of this method is abbreviated as 'sl 1, K2 tog, psso' and the purled version as 'sl 1, P2 tog tbl, psso'.

Working stitches together through the back of the loops

To decrease one knitted stitch at the beginning of a row

Knit the first stitch. Insert the right-hand needle through the *back* loops only of the next two stitches. Knit them both together and drop them off the left-hand needle. The abbreviation for this is 'K2 tog tbl'.

To decrease one knitted stitch at the end of a row

Work until three stitches remain on the left-hand needle. Knit the next

two stitches together through the *back* loops and knit the last stitch.

To decrease one purled stitch at the beginning of a row

Purl the first stitch. Insert the right-hand needle from left to right through the *back* loops only of the next two stitches. Purl them both together and drop them off the left-hand needle. The abbreviation for this is 'P2 tog tbl'.

To decrease one purled stitch at the end of a row work until three stitches remain on the left-hand needle. Purl the next two stitches together through the *back* loops and purl the last stitch.

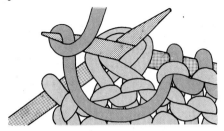

Slip and stitch decreasing

To decrease one knitted stitch at the beginning of a row

Knit the first stitch. Insert the right-hand needle into the next stitch as if to knit it. Keep the yarn at the back of the work and slip the stitch on to the right-hand needle without knitting it. Knit the next stitch on the left-hand needle. Use the left-hand needle to lift the slipped stitch

over the top of the knitted stitch and off the right-hand needle. The abbreviation for this is 'sl 1, K1, psso'.

To decrease two knitted stitches at the beginning of a row

Knit the first stitch. Slip the next stitch and the following stitch on to the right-hand needle. Knit the next

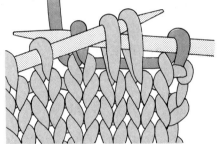

stitch on the left-hand needle. Lift the two slipped stitches over the top of the knitted stitch and off the right-hand needle. The abbreviation of this is 'sl 2, K1, p2sso'.

To decrease one or two purled stitches at the beginning of a row

The yarn must be kept at the front of the work throughout. Slip one or two stitches on to the right-hand needle as if to purl them. Purl the next stitch on the left-hand needle.

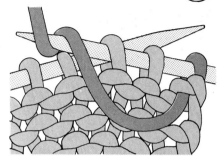

Use the left-hand needle to lift the slipped stitches over the top of the purled stitch and off the right-hand needle. These methods are abbreviated as 'sl 1, P1, psso' and 'sl 2, P1, p2sso'.

Note: To decrease one or two knitted or purled stitches in the middle of a row, work until the position for the decrease is reached. Slip and knit or purl the next two or three stitches as for the beginning of a row.

To decrease one or two knitted or purled stitches at the end of a row, work until three or four stitches remain on the left-hand needle. Work the next two or three stitches as for the beginning of a row and knit or purl the last stitch.

Casting off multiples of stitches

To subtract a number of stitches at the beginning of a knitted row

Cast off the number stated. One stitch remains on the right-hand needle after the casting-off has been completed. This counts as one of the remaining stitches. Continue knitting to the end of the row. The easiest way to subtract a number of stitches at each end of a piece of knitting is to cast off at the beginning of two consecutive rows.

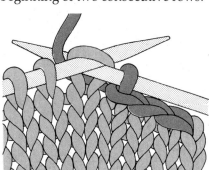

To subtract a number of stitches in the middle of a knitted row

Work until the position for the subtraction is reached. Use the method given for the beginning of a row.

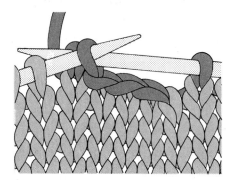

To subtract a number of stitches at the end of a knitted row

Work until the number of stitches to be cast off remains on the left-hand needle. Cast off and fasten off the last stitch. The yarn must be rejoined again at the beginning of the next row to continue knitting. These methods can be used to subtract a number of stitches at the beginning, end or in the middle of a purled row. Purl the stitches instead of knitting them before casting them off.

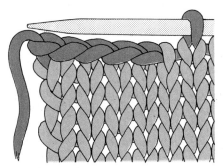

Tension and textures

The importance of tension cannot be underestimated. It makes the difference between knitting a garment successfully from a pattern and producing a jersey which reaches the knees. Also included in this chapter are four more reversible stitches for you to practise and perfect.

Once you can knit stitches you need to know how to obtain accurate measurements of both the length and width of your knitting, in order to follow a pattern. This is called 'tension'. Many knitters mistakenly believe that tension merely means achieving an even fabric. This is not so and you can never be a proficient knitter until you appreciate how important it is to have the correct tension.

The word tension means the number of stitches and rows to a given measurement which has been achieved by the designer, using a specific yarn and needle size. (Each spinner gives a recommended tension for its yarn on the ball band but this is only a guide and is often different from that called for by the pattern.)

A dressmaking pattern tells you how many metres of fabric are needed and this amount stays the same whether the fabric is chiffon or corduroy. However, in knitting the needle size and thickness of yarn have an effect on the number of stitches and rows needed to arrive at a given measurement. Unless you can obtain the tension called for by the pattern you will end up with a garment either too large or too small. Incorrect tension also alters the texture of the fabric.

The basic steps in knitting soon become as natural as breathing but everyone differs in the way they control the needles and yarn. There is no such thing as 'average' tension. Different people naturally knit more tightly or loosely than others. As you become more experienced your tension may alter with your progress.

Checking tension Always work a sample with the correct yarn and needle size in the stitch given before beginning any knitting. If a pattern gives 22 stitches and 30 rows to 10cm/4in worked over stocking stitch on 4mm/No 8 needles, cast on at least 26 stitches. Allow at least 4 extra stitches and 4 extra rows to enable you to measure the sample accurately. Pin the completed sample on a flat surface. Measure with a ruler and count the number of stitches and rows obtained to 10cm/4in. In this example there should be 22 stitches and 30 rows to 10cm/4in.

Don't be tempted to cheat by stretching the sample. Count the stitches and rows very carefully – even half a stitch makes an overall difference.

Adjusting tension If your sample measures *more* than the tension size given you are working too loosely. Change to a size smaller needles and work another sample.

If your sample measures *less* than the tension size given you are working too tightly. Change to larger needles and work another sample.

Continue experimenting with needle sizes until you obtain the tension given. Most instructions give this as a number of stitches in width and a number of rows in depth. If you have to choose between obtaining one but not the other, the width tension is the most vital. If you cannot satisfactorily adapt the tension to obtain the correct width then cast on the number of stitches given for a smaller or larger size. Length can usually be adjusted by working more or less rows.

Always use new yarn for each sample. If you keep on unravelling the same length of yarn it will become stretched and will not give an accurate tension.

Each design is calculated on the tension achieved with the yarn specified in the instructions. The total amount of yarn is also based on the tension. If you choose to use a substitute it is vital to realise that the amount may vary and you may not produce the texture of the original fabric.

Reversible patterns

The three patterns opposite use combinations of knit and purl stitches and form fabrics which look the same on both sides. They can be worked in separate bands or as all-over fabrics. Any of these patterns can be used to knit the bags featured in this chapter.

Moss stitch

Worked over any number of stitches.
1st row *K1, P1, repeat from * to end, noting that an even number of cast-on stitches will end with P1 and an odd number with K1.
2nd row All the stitches of the previous row which were knitted must be knitted and all the purled stitches purled.
These 2 rows form the pattern.

Double moss stitch

This pattern needs a number of stitches which will divide by 4.
1st row *K2, P2, repeat from * to end.
2nd row As 1st.
3rd row *P2, K2, repeat from * to end.
4th row As 3rd.
These 4 rows form the pattern.

Hurdle stitch

This pattern needs an even number of stitches.
1st and 2nd rows K to end.
3rd and 4th rows *K1, P1, repeat from * to end.
These 4 rows form the pattern.

One pattern – two useful bags

To show how tension controls the finished size and texture, this design has been made in two different yarns and needle sizes. The number of stitches and rows remain exactly the same.

Sizes

Holdall 37cm×34cm/14½in×13½in
Shoulder purse 18cm×15cm/7in×6in

You will need

Holdall 10×50g balls of Patons uncut Turkey Rug Wool
One pair 7½mm/No 1 needles
One pair cane handles

Shoulder purse 3×20g balls of Patons Beehive Double Knitting
One pair 4mm/No 8 needles
1m/1yd of cord for handle
1m/1yd decorative tape or ribbon, optional

Tension

Holdall 10 sts and 16 rows to 10cm/4in over moss st worked on 7½mm/No 1 needles

Shoulder purse 19 sts and 34 rows to 10cm/4in over moss st worked on 4mm/No 8 needles

Holdall

With 7½mm/No 1 needles cast on 36 sts by the 2 needle method.
1st row *K1, P1, rep from * to end.
2nd row *P1, K1, rep from * to end.
Work a total of 110 rows moss st. Cast off loosely.

Gussets

With 7½mm/No 1 needles cast on 8 sts. Work 44 rows moss st. Cast off loosely. Make another piece in same way.

Shoulder purse

With 4mm/No 8 needles cast on and work as given for holdall.

Gussets and handle

These are all knitted in one piece. With 4mm/No 8 needles cast on 8 sts. Work 117cm/46in moss st. Cast off loosely.

To make up

Holdall Do not press. Fold bag in half and mark centre of each side with safety pins. Mark centre of cast-on edge of gussets in same way.

Join gussets to bag with a flat seam matching centre markers. Turn right side out. Fold top edges of bag over cane handles and stitch down.
Shoulder purse Do not press. Mark bag and gussets and sew in gussets as given for Holdall. The remainder becomes the handle. Place cord inside the knitted handle length and firmly stitch the open edges together. Thread some decorative tape or ribbon through top edge to tie at front.

Using up tension samples

You need not waste any of your experimental samples as the unravelled yarn can be used up in many ways. One useful tip is to wind

up some of the yarn and attach it to one of the seams of the completed garment. As this will be washed with the garment it will be in the same condition and can be used for darning and repairs. If the yarn is not too thick it can be used for seaming and completing a garment.

Another way of using up yarn is to make a trimming such as a plaited tie-belt for a jersey or a pompom for a pull-on hat.

Borders and edges

Borders and neck edges are usually worked after the pieces have been sewn together — which entails picking up stitches along a cast-off row or on row ends. The secret of a perfect finish is to pick them up evenly.

Front borders are needed on garments which have a centre front opening. A turned-under border in stocking stitch can be worked in one with the main fabric of a jacket but only when the pattern for the body of the jacket is of a similar texture. Garter stitch, for example, should not be worked in the same row with stocking stitch, because garter stitch stretches widthways and stocking stitch lengthways.

A cardigan is usually best finished with separately knitted button and buttonhole borders, which are sewn on when the garment is completed. **Edges** along which stitches have to be picked up are commonly used to complete garments. This method is used to pick up stitches round the curve of a neckline to work a neckband or collar.

A zip-fastened jacket also has stitches picked up along the front edges to neaten them, before the zip is sewn in place; these must be picked up evenly to avoid stretching or puckering the edge.

Turned-under front borders

Right: Once you turn up the picot hem and begin to seam it, you can see how the row of eyelet holes forms a dainty edge.

Make provision for the border before casting on. Decide on the width of the turned-under part – 3-4cm/1¼-1½in will be sufficient but it will depend on the thickness of the yarn being used. If buttonholes are to be worked, allow sufficient width for a double buttonhole, one in the top part of the border and a corresponding one in the under part.

Cast on required number of stitches. The example shown here is worked over 66 stitches. Double knitting yarn on 4mm/No 8 needles is used to give a tension of 22 stitches and 30 rows to 10cm/4in. This allows for 8 stitches to be turned under,

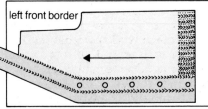

left front border

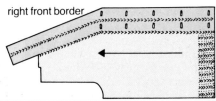

right front border

one foldline stitch and 8 stitches for the upper part of the border, with the remaining 49 stitches being used for the body.

To work a left front border

With the right side of the work facing, work in pattern to the last 17 stitches. Work 8 stitches for the top border, slip the next stitch in a purlwise direction to mark the foldline, knit the last 8 stitches for the turned-under part of the border. On the next row, purl the first 9 stitches, then pattern to the end of the row. Repeat these rows for the required length.

Any shaping on the front edge is worked *before* the top border stitches on a right side row.

To work a right front border

With the right side of the work facing, knit the first 8 stitches for the turned-under border section, slip the next stitch purlwise to mark the foldline, work 8 stitches for the top border then pattern to the end of the row. On the next row, pattern to the last 9 stitches then purl to the end. Repeat these rows

for the required length.

Any shaping on the front edge is worked *after* the top border stitches on a right side row.

Separate front borders

Decide on the width of the border as for turned-under borders. If buttonholes are to be worked, allow one extra stitch on the inner edge of the border so that the buttonhole is central when the border is sewn in position.

To work a border in the same pattern as the welt of the body, such as ribbing, cast on the required number of stitches for the body plus the stitches for the border. Work until the welt is completed.

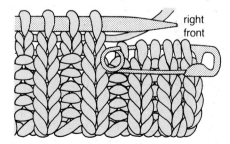

right
front

On the right front With the right side of the work facing, work across the border stitches and slip them on to a holder. Continue in pattern on the remaining stitches.

On the left front With the right side of the work facing, work until the border stitches remain and slip them on to a holder. Turn and continue in pattern on the remaining stitches.

When the main piece is completed put the border stitches back on to the same size needle as used for the welt, rejoin the yarn at the inner edge and continue in pattern. *Work about 10cm/4in and tack the border in place along the front edge, easing this in very slightly as you do so – take care not to stretch the main fabric or the border will pucker. Continue from the * until the border is the required length, then cast off. Stitch the border in place along the edge and remove the tacking stitches.

To work a border in a different pattern to the welt, cast on the border stitches separately. Work in pattern until the border is the required length. Continue from the * as given for working a border in the same pattern.

Picking up stitches evenly

Unless picked-up stitches are evenly spaced, the edge will stretch or pucker. It is a simple matter to pick up stitches along a cast-off row but not so easy to gauge where to pick up stitches on row ends. The picked up edge needs to be very slightly shorter than the main fabric edge.

1 As a general guide, pick up a

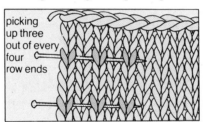

picking up three out of every four row ends

stitch on three out of every four successive row ends.

2 If ribbing is to be worked along the edge, it tends to pull up a little from the bottom edges. To overcome this, pick up a stitch on every row end for the first 5cm/2in of the bottom edge.

Round a neck divide edge into equal sections with pins (the back neck stitches have usually

been cast off or left on a holder). As an example, if a total of 180 stitches are to be picked up round the front of a V-neck, divide each front edge into nine equal sections. Pick up 10 stitches in each section. This avoids the stitches being too bunched together or too far apart.

Picking up edge stitches with a knitting needle

To pick up stitches along a cast-off row, have the right side of the fabric facing you, and a ball of yarn. *Insert the needle from the front to the back under both loops at the top of the cast-off stitch, put the yarn round the needle and pull this loop through, as when working a knit stitch. Leave the stitch on the needle. Continue from the * until the required number of stitches have been picked up using the main

along a cast-off row

length of yarn to make the stitches.

To pick up stitches along row ends, have the right side of the fabric facing you, and a ball of yarn.

1 *Insert the needle from the front to the back between the first and

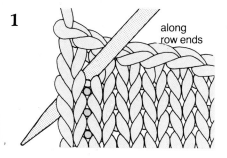

1

along row ends

second stitches in from the edge of the knitting.

2 Put the yarn round the needle and pull this loop through as when working a knit stitch. Leave the stitch on the needle. Insert the needle between the first and second

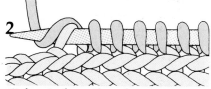

2

stitches in from the edge one row along to the left and continue from the * until the required number of stitches have been picked up using the main length of yarn to make the stitches.

To pick up stitches round a shaped edge, such as a neckline, combine the methods of picking up stitches along a cast-off row and along row ends.

Picking up edge stitches with a crochet hook

To pick up stitches along a cast-off row, or along row ends, work as given for picking up stitches with a knitting needle. Use a crochet hook

to pull the loop through instead of a needle.

1 Insert the crochet hook under the top of the stitch or into the row end, and put the yarn round the hook.

1

2 Pull the loop through.

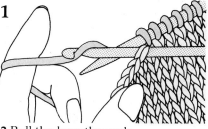

2

3 Transfer the loop from the crochet hook to a knitting needle.

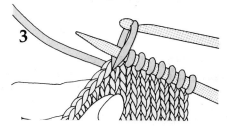

3

Basic making up: blocking, pressing and seaming

Care taken in the final stages of finishing the pieces of a garment and in the actual making up will give your knitting that professional look. Some modern yarns need careful handling and often a garment can be ruined by incorrect pressing or cobbled seams.

The final preparation and making up of a garment needs as much care and skill as the knitting. The knowledge and time taken to produce a superb piece of knitting to the correct shape and proportions can be wasted if the pieces are badly seamed together or if you don't take the trouble to block and press the pieces where appropriate.

Blocking is the term given to the process of pinning out each individual piece of knitting to the correct size and shape, prior to pressing. Some patterns have a tendency to shrink in width and stretch in length. Others may have a slight bias which needs correction, or scalloped edges which must be pinned into shape. Delicate lace patterns often only need blocking out and leaving under a damp cloth for a few hours, without actually pressing them.

Diagrams of the pattern pieces give you the finished measurements of each piece and the making up instructions tell you whether or not to press the yarn. The choice of blocking out the pieces, however, will often be left to you. If you are in any doubt, *do not block* – knitting is a wonderfully pliant fabric and will eventually take its own shape.

Pressing is not always essential or even advisable. In the past, knitters did not press any pure wool garments but 'dressed' them over the steam of a kettle, then patted them into size and shape.

The ballband usually tells you if the yarn can be pressed and gives you the iron temperature setting but does not always give you exact details.

If you use a different yarn from the one specified in the pattern, don't forget that the making up instructions may not be appropriate. The instructions may be for a yarn, such as wool, that *can* be pressed but you may have used acrylic which *cannot* be pressed.

Many yarns are blends of man-made fibres so it is not always easy to judge whether they should be pressed.

If you are in any doubt about a yarn, *do not press*.

Seaming is particularly important for a professional finish. The method you use will depend on the fabric and type of garment. Ribbing and garter stitch should be joined with over-sewn and flat seams, see page 20.

Backstitch seams are suitable for closely-textured fabrics, such as stocking stitch, and for all shaped edges.

The invisible seam resembles the rungs of a ladder, lacing the pieces together. It is perfect for joining straight edges in any pattern and cannot be detected on a stocking stitch seam – hence its name.

Whichever method of seaming you use, assemble all the pieces in the order given in the instructions. Make sure that stripes or patterns match exactly when pinning the edges together. Use a blunt-ended sewing needle and the original yarn. If it is very thick or textured, use a finer matching yarn.

Blocking pattern pieces

To block out each piece you will need a firm table or ironing board. On top of this place a sheet of white carton cardboard. Over this place an ironing pad or blanket.

Place each individual piece right side down on to the prepared ironing board or table. Anchor the piece at each corner with rustless pins. Use a tape measure to check that the width and length are the same as those given in the instructions, when measured in the centre. Gently pat the piece into

shape where any increasing or decreasing has been worked and check the measurements, making sure that the side edges are the same length.

Now pin the piece to the board all round the edges. Use plenty of pins evenly spaced and placed at right angles to the stitches and rows. Take great care to ensure that all the stitches and rows lie in straight lines and that the fabric does not have any bias.

If the pieces need blocking but do not require any pressing, cover them with a clean wet cloth, well wrung out. Leave for two or three hours then remove the cloth.

Pressing

If the individual pieces have not already been blocked, lay them right side down on to an ironing board.

1 Have the iron at the correct temperature and a clean dry, or damp, pressing cloth as directed. Place the cloth over the piece. Gently but firmly press the whole area of the iron down on top of the cloth, then lift it up again. Do not move the iron over the surface of

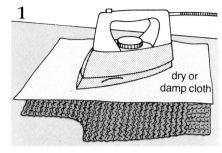

1

dry or damp cloth

the cloth as you would when ironing normally. Press each area evenly in this way before going on to the next area.

Once a piece has been pressed, allow any steam to evaporate. Remove the pins if the piece has been blocked and lay it aside ready for seaming.

2 To steam press a piece, use an iron at the correct temperature setting.

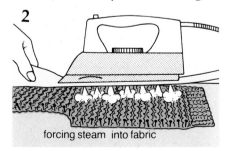

2

forcing steam into fabric

Place a damp cloth over the piece. Begin at the lower edge and hold the left-hand side of the damp cloth just above the surface of the knitting with the left hand. Allow the iron to come into direct contact with the cloth but do not press down on to the knitting. This forces the steam down into the fabric. Press each area in this way.

Once a piece has been pressed allow any steam to evaporate. Remove the pins if the piece has been blocked and lay it aside ready for seaming.

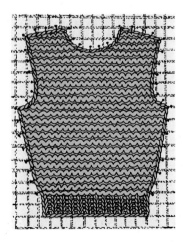

Knitting in rounds

Knitting on sets of needles pointed at each end, or on a circular needle, produces seamless, tubular fabrics. You do not turn at the end of each row as in knitting with pairs of needles, so the right side is always facing you, which affects the methods of working even basic patterns.

Knitting in rounds is the ideal way of making socks, gloves, hats, skirts, or anything that would be spoiled by a bulky seam. Jerseys can also be knitted in the round up to the underarms, then divided and continued in rows as normal – in fact this is how traditional Aran and Guernsey designs are knitted.

You can knit in rounds with either a set of needles – four, five or six – or a circular needle. (Circular needles can also be used to work to and fro in rows.)

When you are knitting in rounds remember that the right side of the fabric is always facing you as you do not turn to begin another row. If you are working a pattern, the method will be different from when knitting in rows, though the result will be the same.

The miniature leaf pattern, used on the bolster cushion in this chapter, is given in rounds. Using this as a guide you can adapt other patterns in the same way by always knitting the second and every alternate row instead of purling it.

Use your preferred method of casting on and if you need to join in a new ball, *splice* the ends of the old and new yarns together.

To cast on with four needles

When you are knitting, the stitches will be divided more or less equally between three needles.

1 Using the method you prefer, you can cast the right number of stitches on to each of the three needles to start with, but be careful that they don't get twisted round the needle before you begin to knit.

An easier method for a small number of stitches is to cast them all on to one needle. Work one or two rows in your pattern, then divide and transfer them to the second and third needles. This way you avoid the stitches getting twisted round the needles, but you will have a gap at the beginning of the work. Use a

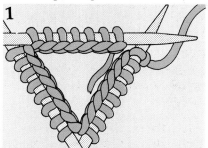

blunt-ended sewing needle and the cast-on end of yarn to join this with a few oversewn stitches.

2 Arrange the three needles in a triangle and use the fourth to begin knitting in rounds.

2

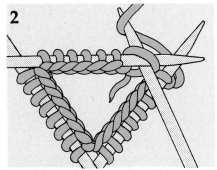

Work across the stitches of the first needle, then use this to work across the stitches of the second needle, and so on. Always pull the yarn tightly across to the first stitch on each needle to avoid a loose stitch.

To cast on with a circular needle

Use the ends of the needle as a pair to cast on the number of stitches required with the method you prefer. Make sure the stitches do not become twisted round the nylon strip which joins the needle ends together. To knit in rounds use the right-hand needle point to work across all the cast-on stitches until you come to the beginning of the round again.

Alternatively, after casting on, turn and use the circular needle as a pair of needles, working the first row without joining it into a round. This is an easier method because it prevents the stitches becoming twisted round the nylon strip, but it does leave a gap in the work. Continue knitting in rounds and join the gap at the beginning with a

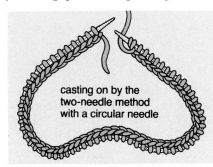

casting on by the two-needle method with a circular needle

few oversewn stitches.
Circular needles are sold in different lengths, to accommodate varying numbers of cast on stitches. The chart on the right lists the minimum number of stitches to cast on for each length of needle, to ensure that you can reach from one needle point to the other without stretching the fabric.

Simple patterns knitted in the round

It is easy to convert simple patterns for knitting in the round. Here are the basic ones most often used.
Stocking stitch Work by knitting every round. This simplifies knitting multi-coloured patterns such as Fair Isle.
Garter stitch Work by knitting the first and every odd-numbered round. The second and every even-numbered round must be purled. Alternate rounds of knitting and

purling form the ridged effect.
Single ribbing Work by alternately knitting and purling one stitch on the first round. If you begin a round with one knitted stitch you must end with one purled stitch to complete the round exactly. On every following round all the knitted stitches are knitted and the purled stitches purled.

Single moss stitch Work by alternately knitting and purling one stitch on the first and every odd-numbered round. If you begin a round with one knitted stitch you must end with one purled stitch to complete the round exactly. In the second and every even-numbered round, the knitted stitches must be purled and purled stitches knitted.

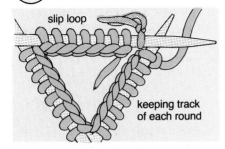

slip loop

keeping track of each round

Note:

It is easy to lose track of the beginning of each round, whether you are using sets of needles or a circular needle. Mark this point by making a slip loop in a length of different coloured yarn and put it on the needle at the beginning of the first round. Slip the loop from one needle point to the other on every round without working into it.

To cast off in rounds

If you are using a set of four needles, use the free needle to cast off the stitches on the first needle of the round until one stitch remains on the right-hand needle. Put aside the left-hand needle. Use the right-hand needle to cast the stitches off the second needle, and so on.

When you get to the very last stitch, fasten off.

If you are using a circular needle, use the right-hand needle point to work the stitches and the left-hand needle point to lift them over and off the needle. When one stitch remains, fasten off.

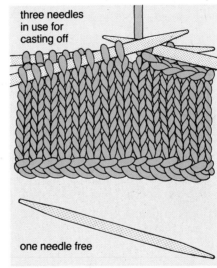

three needles in use for casting off

one needle free

Minimum no of stitches required for circular needles

Tension (sts to 2.5cm/1in)	Needle length			
	40cm 16in	60cm 24in	80cm 30in	100cm 40in
5	80	117	157	196
5½	88	129	173	216
6	96	141	189	236
6½	104	153	205	255
7	112	164	220	275
7½	120	176	236	294
8	128	188	252	314
8½	136	200	268	334
9	144	212	284	353

Bolster up your sofa

Size

57cm/22in long by 49cm/20in circumference (stretch on to pad)

You will need

6×25g balls of Sunbeam Mohair, (67% mohair, 28% wool, 5% nylon)

One 5½mm/No 5 circular needle, 40cm/16in long or set of four 5½mm/No 5 needles

Bolster cushion pad 46cm/18in long × 56cm/22in circumference

Tension

16 sts and 21 rounds to 10cm/4in worked on 5½mm/No 5 needles

To make the cover

Cast on 78 sts and join into a round. K one round. Commence miniature leaf patt.

1st round *K1, yfwd, sl 1, K1, psso, K1, K2 tog, yfwd, rep from * to end.

2nd and 4th rounds K to end.

3rd round *K2, yfwd, sl 2 tog, K1, p2sso, yfwd, K1, rep from * to end.

5th round *K1, K2 tog, yfwd, K1, yfwd, sl 1, K1, psso, rep from * to end.

6th round K to last st, leave last st unworked.

7th round *Sl 2 tog noting that first st is unworked st at end of last round, K1, p2sso, yfwd, K3, yfwd, rep from * to end.

8th round K to end.

These 8 rounds form the patt. Rep them 14 times more. Break off yarn, thread through sts, draw up and fasten off securely. Do not press. Place cover over cushion pad. Thread a separate length of yarn through cast on sts, draw up tightly and fasten off securely.

Make two large tassels with shanks and sew one to each end of cover.

Simple eyelets and horizontal buttonholes

It is the attention to such simple details as buttons and buttonholes that can give your knitting a professional finish. This chapter deals with various ways of working single and double horizontal buttonholes on separate bands or turned-under facings.

Knitting patterns usually give instructions as to where to place buttonholes and how many stitches to cast off to achieve the correct width in proportion to the garment, but they rarely give the method for how to work them.

Most buttonholes are worked on a buttonhole band which can be knitted separately or as part of a garment. Separate buttonhole bands are often knitted in ribbing on finer needles than the main fabric to form a firm neat edge. Knitted-in bands are often in stocking stitch when the rest of the garment is in lace or some other pattern not suitable for buttonholes. Sometimes, when a stitch pattern extends right to the edge of a garment, extra stitches are worked along the buttonhole edge to make a facing strip which is turned back when making up.

Facing strips are usually worked in stocking stitch to give minimum bulk but remember, if you are working the main fabric in a lace pattern, the facing strip will show through.

This chapter gives methods for working eyelet and horizontal buttonholes and a way of neatening them.

Simple eyelet buttonholes This

dainty method is ideal for use on baby garments with small buttons. Eyelets are suitable for buttonholes worked on a buttonhole band whether knitted separately or as part of the main fabric.

Horizontal buttonholes There are several different methods of making horizontal buttonholes all based on the same principle – that a given number of stitches are cast off on one row and replaced by stitches cast on again in the same place on the following row.

One thing to remember when working the first cast-off row for a horizontal buttonhole is that the stitch still on the right-hand needle after the casting off has been completed always counts as one of the remaining stitches of the row.

Which method you choose depends on whether your buttonhole band is knitted separately, as part of the main fabric or with a facing strip and on the size of buttonhole you need and the sort of finish you prefer.

If you are knitting a separate buttonhole band horizontally there is a choice of two methods, one for buttonholes across three or fewer stitches and one for larger buttonholes, which need to be neatened at the corners.

If you are knitting a facing strip to turn back behind the opening edge of the garment, choose the method appropriate for the size of buttonhole you are making, remembering that you have to make a double buttonhole, one in the opening edge of the garment, and a corresponding one in the facing strip.

Simple eyelet buttonholes

Knit the buttonhole band until the position for the buttonhole is reached. If working a separate band, always end with a wrong side row. If working the band as part of the main fabric, end at the edge where the buttonhole is required. On the next row work the given number of stitches, usually three or four, to the point where the

buttonhole is needed. Take the yarn over or round the needle to make an

eyelet hole, work the next two stitches together, then work to the end of the row. Work the following row across all stitches.

Small buttonholes for separate bands

This method is suitable for buttonholes across three or fewer stitches.

Knit the buttonhole band until the position for the buttonhole is reached, ending with a wrong side row.

On the next row work the given number of stitches in pattern to the

point where the buttonhole is needed, cast off the required number of stitches, then pattern to the end of the row.

On the following row replace the cast-off stitches in the previous row with the same number of cast-on stitches, turning the needle to cast on.

Large buttonholes for separate bands

This method is suitable for buttonholes across four or more stitches.

Knit the buttonhole band until the position for the buttonhole is reached, ending with a wrong side row.

On the next row work the given number of stitches in pattern to the point where the buttonhole is needed.

Cast off one *fewer* than the number of stitches given for the buttonhole, for example, if you are told to cast off four stitches, cast off three of these. Slip the stitch on the right-hand needle back on to the left-hand needle and knit this together

with the next stitch to complete the total number of stitches required. On the following row cast on one

more than the number of stitches given for the buttonhole, for example, if you are told to cast on four stitches, cast on five instead. On the next row, work to within one stitch of this extra cast-on stitch. Work the next stitch together with the extra cast-on stitch to complete the buttonhole.

Buttonholes for edges with a facing strip

Knit the garment until the position for the buttonhole is reached, ending at the edge where the buttonhole is required.

On the next row work the given number of stitches in pattern to the point where the first buttonhole is needed in the facing strip, cast off the required number of stitches. Pattern to the point where the corresponding buttonhole is needed in the main fabric, cast off the required number of stitches, then pattern to the end of the row. On the following row replace each set of cast-off stitches in the previous row with the same number of cast-on stitches, turning the needle to cast on.

Reinforced buttonholes for all types of buttonhole band

This example has been worked as a separate ribbed band over twelve stitches, with four stitches for the buttonhole.

Knit the buttonhole band in single rib until position for buttonhole is reached, ending with wrong side row.

1 (K1, P1) twice, leave the yarn at the front of the work and sl the next

1

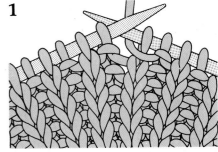

st in a purlwise direction, then take the yarn back between the needles.

2 *Sl the next st on the left-hand needle in a purlwise direction, lift the 2nd st on the right-hand needle over the first st with the point of the

2

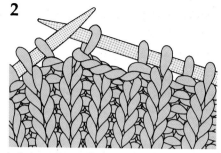

left-hand needle and off the needle, rep from * 3 times more.

3 Sl the last st on the right-hand needle back on to the left-hand needle, turn the work, pick up the yarn and take it to the back of the work.

3

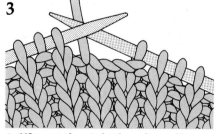

4 **Insert the right-hand needle between the last 2 sts on the left-hand needle and cast on one st, rep from ** 4 times more, turn the work, take the yarn to back of work.

4

5 Sl the last cast-on st on to the left-hand needle, K this st tog with the next st on the left-hand needle to complete the buttonhole, rib to end of row.

5

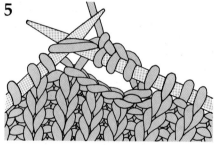

Note: When working the buttonhole row in any other stitch than rib, remember that the yarn must be taken round the first slipped st then left in its correct working position for the stitch prior to the slipped stitch, that is at the back for a knit st and at the front for a purl st.

Choosing buttons

Choose buttons which complement the knitted fabric as well as being practical. Fun shapes look decorative but may have sharp edges that will rub and snag the buttonholes. A man's husky jacket looks best when finished with bold leather or wooden buttons; a crisp cotton cardigan is enhanced by the lustre of real pearl buttons and a lacy evening jacket needs the added sparkle of jewelled buttons.

Consider the thickness of the knitted fabric when choosing buttons. Those with central holes will lie flat on the fabric unless you add a yarn shank but buttons with built-in shanks stand above the fabric to allow for the thickness of the buttonhole band when the buttons are fastened.

Make sure that the buttons you select are the right size to go through the buttonholes without stretching them and that they are the right weight for the fabric – if they are too heavy they will pull the band out of shape.

Positioning buttonholes

Knit the button band first and mark the position of the buttons with pins.

Knit the buttonhole band, working the buttonholes to correspond with these markers. They need to be evenly spaced so that the garment does not gape or pucker so knit the same number of rows between each buttonhole.

Positioning buttons

After making up the garment, pin the buttonhole edge over the button band, matching top and bottom edges and securing these points with pins.

Button-through cardigan in tweed yarn

This classic button-to-the-neck cardigan is lifted into the couture class by the use of beautiful tweed yarn in a range of mouth-watering colours. All the ribbed edges are worked in a plain toning double knitting. The cardigan can be made in six sizes.

Sizes

To fit 86 [91:97:102:107:112]cm/ 34 [36:38:40:42:44]in bust
Length to shoulder, 51 [52:53.5:54.5:56:56]cm/ 20 [20½:21:21½:22:22]in, adjustable
Sleeve seam, 43 [44.5:45.5:45.5:47:47]cm/ 17 [17½:18:18:18½:18½]in adjustable
The figures in [] refer to the 91/36, 97/38, 102/40, 107/42 and 112cm/44in sizes respectively

You will need

6 [6:7:8:8:9]×50g balls of Sirdar Country Style Double Knitting Tweed (61% acrylic, 28% bri-nylon, 11% wool) in main colour A
2×50g balls of Sirdar Country Style plain Double Knitting (45% acrylic, 40% bri-nylon, 15% wool) in contrast colour B
One pair 3¼mm/No 10 needles
One pair 4mm/No 8 needles
Eight buttons

Tension

22 sts and 28 rows to 10cm/4in over st st worked on 4mm/No 8 needles

Back

With 3¼mm/No 10 needles and B
cast on 101 [107:111:117:123:127] sts.
1st row (Rs) K1, *P1, K1, rep from *
to end.
2nd row P1, *K1, P1, rep from * to end.
Rep these 2 rows for 6.5cm/2½in,
ending with a 2nd row. Break off B.
Join in A. Change to 4mm/No 8
needles. Beg with a K row cont in st
st until work measures 30.5cm/12in
from beg, or required length to
underarm, ending with a P row.

Shape armholes

Cast off 6 sts at beg of next 2 rows.
Dec one st at each end of next
5 [5:5:5:7:7] rows, then at each end
of foll 3 [4:4:5:5:6] alt rows.
73 [77:81:85:87:89] sts.
Cont without shaping until
armholes measure
20.5 [21.5:23:24:25.5:25.5]cm/
8 [8½:9:9½:10:10]in from beg,
ending with a P row.

Shape shoulders

Cast off at beg of next and every
row 6 sts 6 times and 4 [5:6:7:7:7] sts
twice. Leave rem 29 [31:33:35:37:39]
sts on holder for centre back neck.

The pattern pieces

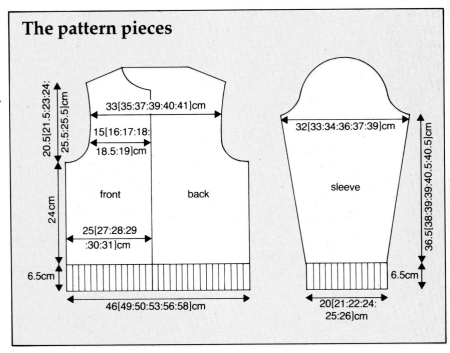

20.5[21.5:23:24:
25.5:25.5]cm

33[35:37:39:40:41]cm

15[16:17:18:
18.5:19]cm

24cm

front   back

25[27:28:29
:30:31]cm

6.5cm

46[49:50:53:56:58]cm

32[33:34:36:37:39]cm

sleeve

36.5[38:39:39:40.5:40.5]cm

6.5cm

20[21:22:24:
25:26]cm

Left front

With 3¼mm/No 10 needles and B
cast on 55 [59:61:63:67:69] sts. Work
6.5cm/2½in rib as given for back.
Break off B. Join in A. Change to
4mm/No 8 needles.
Next row K to last 8 sts, leave last
8 sts on safety pin for front band.
Next row P to end.
47 [51:53:55:59:61] sts.
Beg with a K row cont in st st until
work measures same as back to
underarm, ending at side edge.

Shape armhole

Cast off 6 sts at beg of next row.
Work one row. Dec one st at side
edge on next 5 [5:5:5:7:7] rows, then
at same edge on foll 3 [4:4:5:5:6] alt
rows. 33 [36:38:39:41:42] sts.
Cont without shaping until armhole
measures 14 rows less than back to
shoulder.

Shape neck

Next row Work to last
5 [7:8:8:10:11] sts, leave last
5 [7:8:8:10:11] sts on safety pin for
front neck.
Next row P to end.
28 [29:30:31:31:31] sts.
Dec one st at neck edge on next and
foll 5 alt rows, ending at armhole
edge. 22 [23:24:25:25:25] sts.

Shape shoulder

Cast off at beg of next and every alt
row 6 sts 3 times and 4 [5:6:7:7:7] sts
once.

Right front

With 3¼mm/No 10 needles and B
cast on 55 [59:61:63:67:69] sts. Work
4 rows rib as given for back.
Next row (buttonhole row) Rib 3 sts,
cast off 3 sts, rib to end of row.

Next row Rib to end, casting on 3 sts above those cast off in previous row. Cont in rib until work measures same as left front to end of ribbing, ending at front edge.

Next row Rib 8 sts and leave these on safety pin for front band, change to 4mm/No 8 needles and A, K to end.

Break off B.

Beg with a P row cont in st st and complete as given for left front, reversing all shapings.

Button band

With 3¼mm/No 10 needles and B cast on one st, then with Rs of work facing rib across 8 sts on safety pin. Cont in rib until band, when slightly stretched, fits along left front edge to neck edge, ending with a Ws row. Break off yarn and leave sts on safety pin.

Mark positions for 7 more buttons, last to come in neckband with 6 more evenly spaced between.

Buttonhole band

With 3¼mm/No 10 needles and B cast on one st, then with Ws of work facing rib across 8 sts on safety pin.

Work as given for button band, making buttonholes as before as markers are reached, ending at front edge. Do not break off yarn.

Sleeves

With 3¼mm/No 10 needles and B cast on 43 [45:49:53:55:57] sts. Work 6.5cm/2½in rib as given for back. Break off B. Join in A. Change to 4mm/No 8 needles.

Beg with a K row cont in st st inc one st at each end of 7th and every foll 6th row until there are 71 [73:75:79:81:85] sts.

Cont without shaping until work measures 43 [44.5:45.5:45.5:47:47]cm/ 17 [17½:18:18:18½:18½]in from beg, or required length to underarm, ending with a P row.

Shape top

Cast off 6 sts at beg of next 2 rows. Dec one st at each end of next 5 [5:5:5:5:7] rows, then at each end of every foll alt row until 25 [25:25:27:27:29] sts rem. Work one row.

Cast off at beg of next and every

row 3 sts 6 times and 7 [7:7:9:9:11] sts once.

Neckband

Join shoulder seams. With 3¼mm/ No 10 needles and Rs of work facing, pick up B and rib across sts of right front band, 5 [7:9:8:10:11] sts on safety pin, pick up and K16 sts up right front neck, K29 [31:33:35:37:39] sts on back neck holder, pick up and K16 sts down left front neck, rib across 5 [7:9:8:10:11] sts on safety pin and sts of left front band. 89 [95:99:101:107:111] sts. Beg with a 2nd row work 2.5cm/1in rib as given for back. Cast off in rib.

To make up

Press each piece under a dry cloth with a warm iron. Sew front bands in place. Set in sleeves. Join side and sleeve seams. Sew on buttons.

Neckbands and collars for straight and round necks

Allow sufficient room at the neckline in order to get a garment comfortably over the head.

Details for working the neck of a garment are usually given in full in the instructions but it is also a simple matter to adapt the style of a neckline or collar to suit your preference.

Basic neck shapes are straight across, round, square and V-shaped – either at back, front or both. On all of these shapes you can add front or back vertical openings.

The neatest way to complete the edge is by knitting a neckband or collar in one to avoid uncomfortable seams round the neckline. For all neck shapes except for the straight across neck stitches must be picked up round the edges (page 48), to add the neckband or collar.

To complete a straight neck without a vertical opening, work across the stitches that remain once the shoulder shaping on the back and front is completed. The shoulders and neckband seams are then joined in one, leaving an opening wide enough to pull on easily over the head.

Where a vertical opening is desired at back or front, the piece will have to be divided and each side completed separately, making provision for button and buttonhole bands if required.

To complete a round neck when working on two needles in rows, provision for turning the needles must be allowed.

On a single thickness round neck, a double thickness crew neck or polo collar, seam one shoulder before picking up the neckband stitches, leaving other shoulder unseamed until neckband is completed.

If working single rib in rows, pick up an odd number of stitches and begin and end each row with the same stitch to allow for seaming. If working variations of rib, or in a pattern, make sure you have the correct multiples, plus any edge stitches needed to make the pattern begin and end with the same stitches.

When working single rib on four needles, in rounds, pick up an even number of stitches to ensure the rounds work out exactly. If working in variations of rib or pattern, make sure you have the exact multiples of stitches.

To complete a round-necked collar a centre front or back opening must be left as part of the main fabric, to be closed with a zip or buttons. The collar is worked in rows on two needles and both shoulders can be seamed before picking up the stitches round the neck.

With a centre front overlapped placket opening, a collar is worked in one piece but with a centre back opening, a collar is usually worked in two halves unless the pattern suggests otherwise.

All the examples have been worked in double knitting yarn on 4mm/No 8 needles, using a contrast colour to show the neckline.

Straight necks

Straight neck without opening
Do not work any neck shaping on the back or front.
Work the shoulder shaping as given on the back and
front but do not cast off the remaining neck stitches.
Work a few rows in garter stitch or ribbing across the
neck stitches to give the depth of neckband required.
Cast off.

Round necks

Single round neck in rib
With the right side of the work facing, pick up and knit
the required number of stitches round the neck.
Work in rib for 2cm/¾in, or depth required. **
Cast off loosely.

Double crew neck in rib
Work as given for single round neck to **.
Continue in rib for a further 2cm/¾in, or same depth
as first part. Cast off loosely. Fold neckband in half to
wrong side and slipstitch in place.

Polo neck in rib

Work as given for single round neck to **.
Continue in rib for a further 12cm/4¾in, or total length required. Cast off loosely.
Fold neckband in half to right side.

Finishing a double crew neck

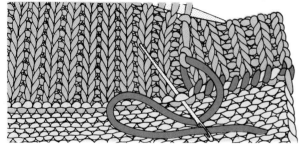

If a double width round neckband without any openings is folded in half to the inside and stitched in place too tightly, it is often difficult to pull the garment over the head – this is particularly uncomfortable for a baby.
The way to overcome this and give a really elastic neckband is to leave the stitches on a separate length of yarn once the length of neckband has been completed, instead of casting them off. The *loops* are then sewn in place and will stretch to allow the garment to be put on, reverting to the snug fit of the neckband in wear.
Thread a blunt-ended sewing needle with a length of yarn. Secure this with one or two stitches on top

of each other at the base of the first of the picked-up neckband stitches.
Fold the neckband in half to the inside, insert the sewing needle into the loop at the top of the same stitch on the separate length of thread and pull the yarn through loosely.
*Insert the sewing needle through one strand at the base of the next stitch and pull the yarn through, then insert the needle into the loop at the top of the same stitch on the separate length of thread and pull the yarn through loosely.
Repeat from * until all the loops have been secured.
Fasten off with one or two small stitches on top of each other. Remove the separate length of thread.

Polo-necked jersey

This raglan-sleeved jersey in wide stripes of five colours can be made with a polo collar or crew neckband. To make this design in one colour only, add the quantities together.

Sizes

To fit 86 [91:97]cm/34 [36:38]in bust
Length to centre back neck,
64 [65:66]cm/25¼ [25½:26]in
Sleeve seam, 46cm/18in
The figures in [] refer to the 91/36 and 97cm/38in sizes respectively

You will need

Polo neck version 5 [5:6]×50g balls of Chat Botté Kid Mohair (80% mohair, 20% chlorofibre) in main colour A
Crew neck version 3 [4:4] balls of same in A
Both versions 2 [3:3] balls in contrast colour B
2 [2:2] balls each in contrast colours C, D and E
One pair 5mm/No 6 needles
One pair 6mm/No 4 needles
Set of four 5mm/No 6 needles pointed at both ends

Tension

15 sts and 20 rows to 10cm/4in over st st worked on 6mm/No 4 needles using 2 ends of yarn

Note

Two strands of yarn are knitted together throughout

Back

With 5mm/No 6 needles and 2 strands of A, cast on 70 [74:78] sts.
1st row (Rs) K2, *P2, K2, rep from * to end.
2nd row P2, *K2, P2, rep from * to end.
Rep these 2 rows for 9cm/3½in, ending with a 2nd row. Break off A. Change to 6mm/No 4 needles and 2 strands of B. Beg with a K row cont in st st, working 18 rows each in B, C and D, then 14 rows with E, ending with a P row.

Shape armholes

Next row With E, K1, K2 tog, K to last 3 sts, sl 1, K1, psso, K1.
Next row With E, P to end.
Rep last 2 rows once more. Break off E.
Cont rep last 2 rows until 28 [30:32] sts rem, working 18 rows with A then cont with B to end.

Leave rem sts on holder.

Front

Work as given for back until 36 [38:40] sts rem in armhole shaping, ending with a P row.

Shape neck

Next row Keeping stripes correct throughout, K1, K2 tog, K10 sts, turn and leave rem sts on holder. Complete left side first.
Next row Cast off 2 sts at neck edge, P to end.
Next row K1, K2 tog, K to end.
Rep last 2 rows twice more.
Next row P2 tog, P1.
Cast off rem 2 sts.
With Rs of work facing leave first 10 [12:14] sts on holder for centre front neck, rejoin yarn to rem sts, K to last 3 sts, sl 1, K1, psso, K1.
Complete to match first side, reversing shapings.

Sleeves

With 5mm/No 6 needles and 2 strands of A, cast on 34 sts. Work 9cm/3½in rib as given for back, ending with a 1st row.
Next row (inc row) Rib 4 [5:7] sts, *pick up loop lying between needles and K tbl – **called M1**, rib 26

[8:4] sts, rep from * 0 [2:4] times more, M1, rib 4 [5:7] sts. 36 [38:40] sts.

Change to 6mm/No 4 needles. Beg with a K row work 6 rows st st. Break off A. Join in 2 strands of B. Cont in st st, working stripes as given for back, inc one st at each end of 5th and every foll 10th row until there are 48 [50:52] sts. Cont without shaping until 14 rows in E have been completed, thus ending with same row as back at underarms.

Shape top

Work as given for armhole shaping on back until 6 sts rem, ending with a P row.
Leave sts on holder.

Polo neck version

Join raglan seams. With Rs of work facing, set of four 5mm/No 6 needles and 2 strands of A, K across sts of back neck and left sleeve K2 tog at seam, pick up and K12 sts down left front neck, K across front neck sts on holder, pick up and K12 sts up right front neck, then K across sts of right sleeve K last st tog with first st of back. 72 [76:80] sts.

Cont in rounds of K2, P2 rib for 24cm/9½in. Cast off very loosely in rib.

Crew neckband

Join raglan seams. With Rs of work facing, set of four 5mm/No 6 needles and 2 strands of A, K across sts of back neck and left sleeve K2 tog at seam, pick up and K8 sts down left front neck, K across front neck sts on holder, pick up and K8 sts up right front neck, then K across sts of right sleeve K last st tog

with first st of back. 64 [68:72] sts. Cont in rounds of K2, P2 rib for 5cm/2in. Leave sts on a separate length of thread.

To make up

Do not press. Join side and sleeve seams. Fold polo neck over to outside.
Fold crew neckband in half to Ws and sl st in place, sewing the loops on the thread to picked up sts of neck and removing the thread as you go.

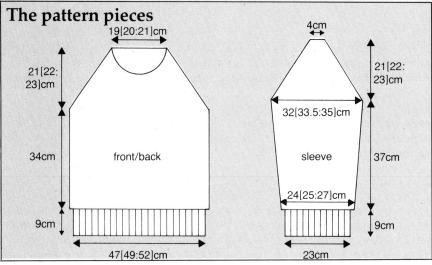

The pattern pieces

19[20:21]cm

21[22:23]cm

34cm

front/back

9cm

47[49:52]cm

4cm

21[22:23]cm

32[33.5:35]cm

sleeve

37cm

24[25:27]cm

9cm

23cm

Neckband variations for square and V necks

Square and V necklines have fewer styles than round necks and, as there is plenty of room to go over the head, they do not usually need a front or back opening. Finish them with a neat ribbed edging worked in rounds, or a picot hem in stocking stitch.

For a better finish work these neckbands in rounds on a set of four needles pointed at both ends or on a circular needle.

These necklines do not usually need front or back vertical openings, except as a decorative feature, as they are wide enough for the average person to get over the head.

To complete a square neckband on a jersey, seam both shoulders before picking up stitches round the neck. To ensure that the neckband sits neatly, all four corners of the square must be mitred.

With a single thickness of ribbing, decrease at each corner to form the mitres. With a double thickness of fabric when the neckband is folded over to form a hem, decrease at each corner on the upper side of the neckband and increase to the original number on the under side.

A heart-shaped neckline is a variation of square with the main fabric at centre front gathered up for about 10cm/4in, pulling the neckband down in the centre. Complete by sewing a separate tab over the gathers.

To complete a V-neckband on two needles, join one shoulder seam only, before picking up the stitches. This enables the work to be turned after each row.

If working single rib in rows, pick up an odd number of stitches and begin and end each row with the same stitch to allow for seaming. If working in a pattern, make sure you have the correct multiples plus any edge stitches needed to ensure that the pattern begins and ends with the same stitches.

When working single rib in rounds, pick up an even number of stitches, or exact multiples if working a pattern to ensure the rounds work out correctly.

To ensure that the neckband sits correctly, decrease stitches on each side of the centre point of the V. Mark the centre front stitch with a length of contrasting coloured yarn as a guide to shaping.

For a variation work the neckband without any shaping and complete by overlapping one centre front edge over the other depending whether it is for a man or a woman.

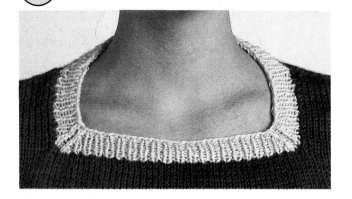

Square neck in single rib

With the right side facing, begin at the back neck and pick up and knit the required number of stitches round the neck.

Work in rounds making sure that you have an odd number of stitches across the back, any number of stitches down the side of the neck, a corner stitch, the same odd number of stitches across the front as for the back, a corner stitch, the same number of stitches up the other side of the neck as for the first side. **

Next round *Rib to within 2 sts of marked corner st, K2 tog, P corner st, sl 1, K1, psso, rep from * once more, rib to end.

Next round Keeping rib correct over dec, rib to end. Repeat these 2 rounds until neckband measures 2.5cm/1in, or required depth ending with a 2nd round. Cast off in rib dec as before. ***

Double V-neck in single rib

With the right side facing pick up and knit the required number of stitches round the neck having an even number and one stitch from the exact centre of the point.

Work in rounds of single rib.

Next round Rib to within 2 sts of centre front st, sl 1, K1, psso, K centre st, K2 tog, rib to end.
Keeping rib correct repeat this round for about 2.5cm/1in, or required depth.

Next round Rib to centre front st, pick up loop lying between needles and K tbl – **called M1**, K centre front st, M1, rib to end.
Keeping rib correct repeat last round for about 2.5cm/1in, or required depth to match first side. Cast off firmly, still increasing at centre front. Fold neckband in half to inside and slipstitch in place.

Heart-shaped neck in single rib

Work as given for square neck in single rib to ***.

Tab

Cast on 2 sts. P one row.

Next row K1, pick up loop lying between needles and K tbl, **called M1**, K1.
Next row P1, K1, P1.
Next row K1, M1, K1, M1, K1.
Next row P1, K1, P1, K1, P1.
Next row K1, M1, rib to last st, M1, K1.
Continue in single rib without shaping for about 7.5cm/3in, or required length to cover gathers less about 2.5cm/1in.
Gather up 10cm/4in of main fabric below neckline at centre front. Sew straight edge of tab to lower edge of neckline. Sew shaped edge of tab at bottom of gathers or fasten down with a button.

A selection of necklines showing a heart-shaped, a V, and a square neck

Square-necked jersey

This stylish jersey is shown here with either a high, square neckline or a lower one, which you can make into a heart-shape.

Sizes

To fit 86–91 [97–102]cm/34–36 [38–40]in bust
Length to shoulder, 57cm/22½in
Sleeve seam, 47cm/18½in
The figures in [] refer to the 97–102cm/38–40in size only

You will need

12 [13] × 50g balls of Scheepjeswol Superwash Zermatt (100% wool)
One pair 3¼mm/No 10 needles
One pair 4mm/No 8 needles
Set of four 3¼mm/No 10 needles pointed at both ends

Tension

21 sts and 29 rows to 10cm/4in over patt worked on 4mm/No 8 needles

Back

With 3¼mm/No 10 needles cast on 101 [111] sts.

1st row (Rs) K1, *P1, K1, rep from * to end.
2nd row P1, *K1, P1, rep from * to end.
Rep these 2 rows for 5cm/2in, ending with a 2nd row and inc one st at end of last row on 2nd size only. 101 [112] sts.
Change to 4mm/No 8 needles. Commence patt.
1st row (Rs) K1, *P1, K10, rep from * to last st, K1.
2nd row K1, *P9, K2, rep from * to last st, K1.
3rd row K1, *P3, K8, rep from * to last st, K1.
4th row K1, *P7, K4, rep from * to last st, K1.
5th row K1, *P5, K6, rep from * to last st, K1.
6th and 7th rows As 5th row.
8th row As 4th.
9th row As 3rd.
10th row As 2nd.
11th row As 1st.
12th row K1, *K1, P10, rep from * to last st, K1.
13th row K1, *K9, P2, rep from * to last st, K1.
14th row K1, *K3, P8, rep from * to last st, K1.
15th row K1, *K7, P4, rep from * to

last st, K1.
16th row K1, *K5, P6, rep from * to last st, K1.
17th and 18th rows As 16th row.
19th row As 15th.
20th row As 14th.
21st row As 13th.
22nd row As 12th.
These 22 rows form the patt and are rep throughout.
Cont in patt until work measures 53cm/20¾in from beg for high neck, or 45cm/17¾in for low neck, ending with a Ws row.

Shape neck

**Next row Patt 30 [35] sts, turn and leave rem sts on holder.
Complete right back shoulder first. Cont without shaping until work measures 57cm/22½in from beg, ending with a Ws row. Cast off. With Rs of work facing return to rem sts on holder, leave first 41 [42] sts for centre back neck, rejoin yarn to rem sts and patt to end. Complete to match first side.

Front

Work as given for back.

Sleeves

With 3¼mm/No 10 needles cast on

The pattern pieces

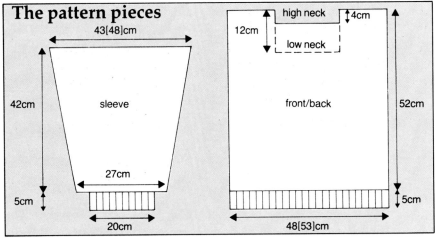

sleeve

43[48]cm

42cm

27cm

5cm

20cm

high neck

12cm

4cm

low neck

front/back

52cm

5cm

48[53]cm

43 sts. Work 5cm/2in rib as given for back, ending with a 1st row.
Next row (inc row) P1, *inc in next st, rib 2 sts, rep from * to end. 57 sts. Change to 4mm/No 8 needles. Cont in patt as given for back, inc one st at each end of 5th and every foll 6th [5th] row, working extra sts into patt, until there are 91 [101] sts. Cont without shaping until sleeve measures 47cm/18½in from beg, ending with a Ws row.
Cast off loosely.

High neckband

Join shoulder seams.
With Rs of work facing and set of four 3¼mm/No 10 needles, *K across back neck sts on holder inc 2 [1] sts evenly, pick up and K19 sts evenly along side edge of neck, rep from * round front neck and along other side. 124 sts.
Next round *K1, P1, rep from * to end.
Next round (shape corners) K1, P2 tog, rib 37 sts, *P2 tog, K1, P2 tog *, rib 15 sts, rep from * to *, rib 37 sts, rep from * to *, rib 15 sts, P2 tog.

Next round (K1, rib 39 sts, K1, rib 17 sts) twice.
Work 4 more rounds in rib, dec at corners as before on next and foll alt round.
Cast off in rib still dec at corners.

Low neckband

Join shoulder seams.
With Rs of work facing and set of four 3¼mm/No 10 needles, *K across back neck sts on holder inc 2 [1] sts evenly, pick up and K57 sts along side edge of neck, rep from * round front neck and along other side. 200 sts.
Next round *K1, P1, rep from * to end.
Next round (shape corners) K1, P2 tog, rib 37 sts, *P2 tog, K1, P2 tog *, rib 53 sts, rep from * to *, rib 37 sts, rep from * to *, rib 53 sts, P2 tog, K1.
Next round (K1, rib 39 sts, K1, rib 55 sts) twice.
Complete as given for high neckband.

To make up

Do not press. Set in sleeves with centre to shoulder seams. Join side and sleeve seams. Press seams lightly under a wet cloth with warm iron. Do not flatten pattern.

Inserted pocket techniques

Pockets are a practical and useful addition to a garment and it is easy to add them to a pattern or to change the style to suit your requirements. These inserted pockets can be horizontal, vertical or diagonal and knitted to match the garment fabric.

If you want to use a pattern that does not include inserted pockets, it is a simple matter to add them. A little pre-planning is necessary and you will also need an extra ball of the yarn.

Choose the style of pocket to fit in with the structure of the main fabric and the shape of the garment. Make sure the fabric is suitable so that it will hold the shape of a pocket without sagging. For example, pockets on very lacy fabrics tend to pull out of shape.

The size of the pocket must also be taken into account at the planning stage. A small pocket on a chunky jacket will look out of proportion while a large pocket on a dainty cardigan would look clumsy and sag out of shape.

Inserted pockets can be horizontal or vertical. If they are not included in the instructions you must work out the position for each pocket before beginning to knit.

Calculate the width and depth of pocket needed – on a woman's cardigan in double knitting, 12.5cm/5in square is a good size. The opening must be clear of any shaping and front edges.

If a horizontal pocket is to be placed above a ribbed welt you must work sufficient depth in the main fabric to allow the lower edge of the pocket lining to come at the top of the ribbing. The pocket opening edge looks best neatened with the type of ribbing used on the other edges.

If vertical pockets are to be positioned on the fronts of a jacket, you must allow sufficient width in the main fabric from the pocket opening to ensure that the edges of the lining do not overlap the front edges.

A vertical pouch pocket can be placed on the front of a jersey. The pocket opening edges look best neatened with ribbing, as used on the other edges.

Diagonal inserted pockets Before beginning to knit, decide where the pocket opening is to begin and the direction in which it must slant for the right or left front. The opening must be clear of any shaping and allow for a lining to be sewn above the welt, also without overlapping front edges. The slanting edge of the pocket can be neatened with ribbing, as used on the other garment edges.

On all of the inserted pocket techniques, the pocket lining is slip-stitched into place on completion of the garment.

Horizontal stocking stitch pocket

Check the number of stitches and rows needed to give the correct size. This example is worked over 30 stitches in double knitting yarn on 4mm/No 8 needles on the right front of the cardigan. For any other pattern, make sure the multiples of stitches for the upper side of the pocket will work out exactly. Adjust the number left for the pocket opening and cast on for the lining, as required.

Cast on 30 sts for the inner pocket lining. Beg with a K row cont in st st for the depth of pocket required, ending with a P row. Break off yarn and leave these sts on a holder.

Work the welt or hem as given in the instructions. Cont in the patt for the main fabric to the same depth as the lining, ending with a Ws row.

Next row Work to the position for the opening, sl 30 sts for the pocket opening on to a holder, with Rs of pocket lining sts to the Ws of the main fabric, work across lining sts on holder, then work to end of row. Complete the right front as given in the instructions. With the Rs of the work facing and a size smaller needles, rejoin yarn to the pocket opening sts on holder. Work 2.5cm/1in ribbing. Cast off loosely. Stitch pocket lining in place.

Vertical basket stitch pocket

This example is worked over 32 stitches and 40 rows in double knitting yarn on 4mm/No 8 needles on the left front of a jacket. For any other pattern, check that the position for the pocket opening comes at the end of a repeat of the multiples of stitches.

Work in basket stitch pattern of K4, P4 until lower edge of opening is reached, ending at the side edge.

Next row Patt multiples of 4 sts to the position for the opening, turn and leave rem sts on holder.

Next row Cast on 32 sts for pocket lining, P32 then patt to end.

Keeping pocket lining in st st, work the number of rows over these sts to give the depth of pocket, ending at lining edge.

Next row Cast off 32 sts, patt to end. Do not break off yarn. Return to where the work was divided, join in a separate ball of yarn to rem sts and patt to end. Work the same number of rows as for the first side, ending at pocket opening edge. Break off yarn.

Return to the first section, work across all sts in patt to close the opening. Complete the left front as given in the instructions. Stitch lining in place. With Rs facing and a smaller needle size, pick up and knit sts along edge of pocket. Work 2cm/¾in rib. Cast off in rib.

Vertical stocking stitch pocket

Check the number of stitches and rows needed to give the correct size. This example is worked over 59 stitches and 46 rows in double knitting yarn on 4mm/No 8 needles across the centre front of a jersey. Cast on 59 sts for the inner pocket lining. Beg with a K row work 10 rows st st, or the depth required to reach from the top of the welt to the lower edge of the pocket opening, ending with a P row. Leave sts on a holder. Work the welt as given in the instructions, then beg with a K row and work the same number of rows as worked for the pocket lining.

Next row K to the position for the left-hand pocket opening, sl the next 59 sts on to a thread and leave for the time being, K across the pocket lining sts then K to the end of the row.

Beg with a P row cont in st st for 45 rows, or the required depth of pocket, ending with a P row. Leave sts for time being. Do not break off yarn.

Complete the pocket front by joining in a separate ball of yarn to the sts left on the thread and work the same number of rows as for the first piece. Break off the yarn.

Return to where the yarn was left and join the pocket front and lining.

Next row K to the pocket opening, place the sts of the pocket front in front of the main fabric and K together one st from each needle until all the sts have been worked, then K to end.

Complete the front as given in the instructions. With the Rs of the work facing and a smaller needle

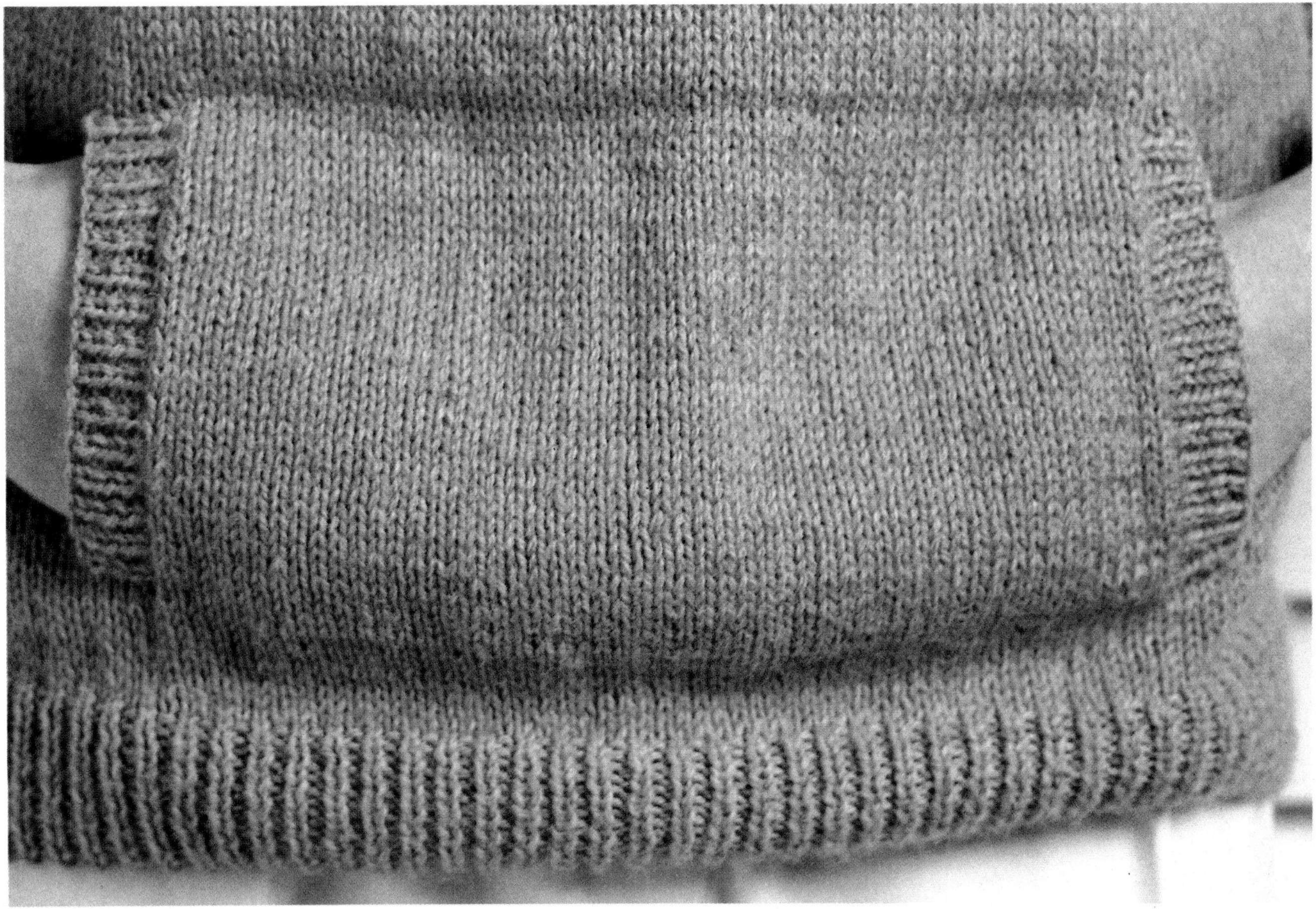

size, pick up and knit the required number of stitches along the left-hand edge of the pocket front. Work 2cm/¾in ribbing. Cast off.
Work along the right-hand edge of the pocket front in the same way.
Stitch base of pocket lining in place.

Diagonal stocking stitch pocket

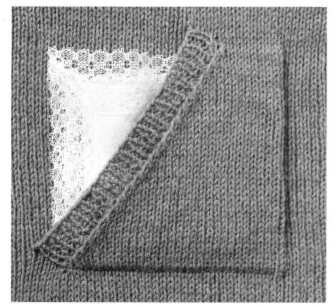

Check where the lower edge of the pocket opening is to begin and the way in which it must slant. This example is worked over 30 stitches in double knitting yarn on 4mm/No 8 needles on the right front of a jacket and slants from left to right.
Work the welt or hem as given in the instructions. Beg with a K row cont in st st until the lower edge of the opening has been reached, ending with a P row.

Next row Work to the position for the opening, turn. Leave remaining stitches on holder.
Dec one st at beg of next row and at same edge on every alt row 30 times in all, ending at front edge. Do not break off yarn.

With separate ball of yarn cast on 30 sts for pocket lining and use this yarn to complete other side of pocket opening.
Beg with a K row cont in st st to give depth of pocket from top edge of welt to lower edge of opening, ending with a K row.

Continue to knit across stitches on holder to end of row. Cont in st st until same number of rows have been worked as for first side, omitting dec, ending with a P row. Break off yarn.
Return to the first section, work across stitches, knitting together one stitch from each needle to join pocket top to main fabric. Complete the right front as given in the instructions.

Complete as given for basket st vertical pocket.
Stitch pocket lining in place.

Raglan-sleeve jersey with pouch pocket

This classic crew-neck jersey in stocking stitch, is quick and easy to knit. The pouch pocket is ideal for keeping hands warm on cold winter days and adds an attractive feature to an otherwise plain garment. All the ribbing is knitted in a contrast colour.

Sizes

To fit 81 [86:91:97:102:107]cm/ 32 [34:36:38:40:42]in bust/chest
Length to centre back neck, 56 [57:58:59:60:61]cm/ 22 [22½:22¾:23¼:23½:24]in
Sleeve seam, 43 [44:45:46:47:48]cm/ 17 [17¼:17¾:18:18½:19]in
The figures in [] refer to the 86/34, 91/36, 97/38, 102/40 and 107cm/42in sizes respectively

You will need

6 [7:7:8:8:9]×50g balls of Hayfield Grampian Double Knitting (45% acrylic, 40% Bri-nylon, 15% wool) in main colour A
1 [1:1:1:2:2] balls of same in contrast colour B
One pair 3¼mm/No 10 needles
One pair 4mm/No 8 needles
Set of four 3¼mm/No 10 needles pointed at both ends

Tension

22 sts and 30 rows to 10cm/4in over st st worked on 4mm/No 8 needles

Back

With 3¼mm/No 10 needles and B cast on 99 [105:111:117:123:129] sts.
1st row (Rs) K1, *P1, K1, rep from * to end.
2nd row P1, *K1, P1, rep from * to end.
Rep these 2 rows for 5cm/2in, ending with a 2nd row. Break off B. **
Change to 4mm/No 8 needles. Join in A. Beg with a K row cont in st st until work measures 36cm/14¼in from beg, ending with a P row.

Shape raglan armholes

Cast off 5 sts at beg of next 2 rows.
Next row K1, sl 1, K1, psso, K to last 3 sts, K2 tog, K1.
Next row P to end.
Rep last 2 rows until
31 [33:35:37:39:41] sts rem, ending with a P row.
Leave sts on holder for centre back neck.

Front

With 4mm/No 8 needles and A cast on 55 [55:57:57:59:59] sts for pocket lining. Beg with a K row work 10 rows st st. Leave sts on holder.
Work front as given for back to **.
Change to 4mm/No 8 needles. Join in A. Beg with a K row work 10 rows st st.

Place pocket

Next row K22 [25:27:30:32:35] sts, sl next 55 [55:57:57:59:59] sts on to a thread and leave for time being, K across pocket lining sts, K to end. Beg with a P row cont in st st for 13 [13:14:14:15:15]cm/ 5 [5:5½:5½:6:6]in, ending with a P row. Leave sts for time being. Do not break off yarn.

Complete pocket front

With Rs of work facing and 4mm/ No 8 needles, join in another ball of yarn to sts on thread and work to match length of first piece, ending with a P row.
Break off yarn. Leave sts on needle.

Join pocket front and lining

Next row With Rs facing return to where yarn was left,
K22 [25:27:30:32:35] sts, place sts of pocket front in front of work and K tog one st from each needle until all sts are worked, then K rem 22 [25:27:30:32:35] sts.
Cont as given for back until 49 [51:53:55:57:59] sts rem in raglan armhole shaping, ending with a P row.

Shape neck

Next row K1, sl 1, K1, psso, K14 sts, turn and leave rem sts on spare needle.
Next row P to end.
Next row K1, sl 1, K1, psso, K to last 3 sts, sl 1, K1, psso, K1.
Rep last 2 rows 5 times more, then dec at armhole edge only on foll 2 alt rows.
Cast off rem 2 sts.
With Rs of work facing, sl first 15 [17:19:21:23:25] sts on to holder, rejoin yarn to rem sts, K to last 3 sts, K2 tog, K1.
Next row P to end.
Next row K1, K2 tog, K to last 3 sts, K2 tog, K1.
Complete to match first side.

Sleeves

With 3¼mm/No 10 needles and B cast on 41 [43:45:47:49:51] sts. Work 5cm/2in rib as given for back, ending with a 1st row.

Next row (inc row) Rib 5 [6:5:6:3:4] sts, *pick up loop lying between needles and K tbl – **called M1**, rib 10 [10:7:7:6:6:] sts, rep from * to last 6 [7:5:6:4:5] sts, M1, rib to end. 45 [47:51:53:57:59] sts.

Break off B. Join in A. Change to 4mm/No 8 needles. Beg with a K row cont in st st inc one st at each end of 5th and every foll 8th row until there are 71 [75:79:83:87:91] sts. Cont without shaping until sleeve measures 43 [44:45:46:47:48]cm/ 17 [17¼:17¾:18:18½:19]in from beg, ending with a P row. Place a marker at each end of last row then work a further 6 rows.

Shape top

Next row K1, sl 1, K1, psso, K to last 3 sts, K2 tog, K1.
Next row P to end.
Rep last 2 rows until 13 sts rem, ending with a P row. Leave sts on holder.

Neckband

Join raglan seams, sewing the last 6 rows of sleeves from markers to cast off sts at armholes.

With Rs of work facing, set of four 3¼mm/No 10 needles and B, K across sts of back neck and left sleeve K2 tog at seam, pick up and K10 sts down left front neck, K across front neck sts, pick up and K10 sts up right front neck, then K across sts of right sleeve K last st of sleeve tog with first st of back neck. 90 [94:98:102:106:110] sts.
Cont in rounds of K1, P1 rib for 5cm/2in. Cast off loosely in rib.

Pocket edges

With Rs of work facing, 3¼mm/No 10 needles and B, pick up and K31 [31:35:35:39:39] sts along edge of pocket.
1st row (Ws) K1, *P1, K1, rep from * to end.

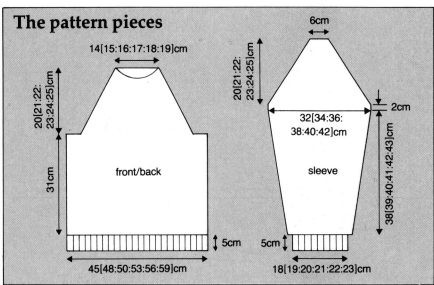

The pattern pieces

14[15:16:17:18:19]cm

20[21:22:23:24:25]cm

31cm

front/back

45[48:50:53:56:59]cm

5cm

6cm

20[21:22:23:24:25]cm

32[34:36:38:40:42]cm

2cm

sleeve

38[39:40:41:42:43]cm

5cm

18[19:20:21:22:23]cm

2nd row P1, *K1, P1, rep from * to end.
Rep these 2 rows for 2cm/¾in. Cast off in rib.

To make up

Press lightly under a dry cloth with a warm iron. Join side and sleeve seams. Sew cast-on edge of pocket lining to top of ribbed welt. Sew

down ends of pocket edges. Fold neckband in half to Ws and sl st in place. Press seams.

DESIGN EXTRA
Patch pockets

This quick and simple method can add pockets to an existing garment as well as to the jersey you are knitting. Buy a ball of yarn in a toning or contrasting colour, or use up oddments of yarn of the same thickness to work jazzy stripes or a Fair Isle motif.

Calculate the width and depth of the pocket using an oddment of fabric pinned to the garment. Make sure the pocket does not interfere with any shaping or overlap edges. Large patch pockets are usually positioned with the lower edge just above the ribbing or hem. Smaller

pockets look effective as breast pockets or as a decorative feature on a sleeve.

Finish the top edge with a few rows of ribbing to match the garment edges or reverse the pattern at the top of the pocket to make a turned down flap.

Apply patch pockets directly on to the garment. Use a fine knitting needle, pointed at both ends, to keep the pocket side edges in line with the main fabric. Pick up every alternate stitch along the line of the main fabric with the needle. Catch one stitch from pocket edge and one from needle alternately.

Work across the row of the main fabric corresponding with the lower edge of pocket in the same way.

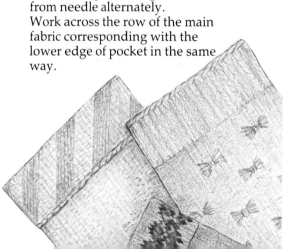

Colouring-book stripes

Incredible it may seem, but every one of the exciting striped patterns in this chapter was created simply by using two or more colours and basic knit or purl stitches. So cue yourself in to colour and transform a basic jersey into a unique design.

Working striped (or checked) patterns is a most enjoyable way of experimenting with colour and, at the same time, using up oddments of the same thickness of yarn.

Horizontal and chevron stripes are particularly easy, as only one colour at a time is used in a row. These patterns produce fabrics of a *single* thickness.

Narrow vertical or diagonal stripes use two colours at a time in a row, and produce fabrics of *double* thickness.

The colours used in all patterns of this type are coded for ease of identification, the first colour as A, the second B, the third C and so on.

Horizontal stripes

In stocking stitch, the knitted side will show an unbroken line of colour and the purl side a broken line.

In garter stitch, if an even number of rows is worked in each colour the right side shows an unbroken line of colour and the wrong side a broken one.

All ribbed stitches can be worked in stripes, but if you wish to keep an unbroken line of colour on the right side, the first row of each new colour must be knitted instead of ribbed. If you work in ribbing throughout, a broken line of colour will show on the right side.

When horizontal stripes are worked over an even number of rows, it is a simple matter to change colours. Whatever the pattern, each new colour is brought into use at the beginning of a row and at the same edge. When working narrow stripes with no more than three colours, the two colours not in use can be carried loosely up the side of the work and twisted round the last colour used before you continue to knit with the next colour.

However, to work more than eight rows in any colour – or in more than three colours – do not carry yarns up the side, as this will pull the side edge out of shape. Instead, break off the yarn at the end of each stripe and rejoin it when it is needed again.

To work horizontal stripes over a random number of rows, use a pair of needles pointed at both ends. Each new colour will not necessarily be joined in at the same edge and working an odd number of rows will leave the yarn at the opposite end of the row.

Random horizontal stripes

Garter stitch stripes

Using A cast on any number of sts.
Work in g st, 3 rows A, 3 rows B,
3 rows C and 3 rows D.
These 12 rows form the pattern.

Stocking stitch stripes

Using A cast on any number of sts.
Work in st st, 2 rows A, 1 row B,
3 rows C, 1 row D, 4 rows E, 1 row
B, 2 rows A, 1 row E and 3 rows D.
These 18 rows form the pattern.

Narrow vertical stripes

Two-colour stripes of this type look
best worked in stocking stitch as this
defines the edge of each stripe.
Stitches are worked with the first and
second colours alternately, changing
at regular points across each row.
The yarn not in use is carried loosely
across the back of the work each time
it is needed. On a knit row carry the
yarn across the back and on a purl
row across the front of the work. Take
the yarn not in use across in the same
position each time – the second colour over the top of the first and the
first colour under the second. Do not
pull the yarn across tightly or you will
pucker the fabric.

Using A cast on multiples of 6 sts
plus 3, eg 27. Work in st st.
1st row (Rs) Keeping yarn at back,
K3 A, *K3 B, K3 A, rep from * to end.
2nd row Keep yarn at front, P3 A,
*P3 B, P3 A, rep from * to end.
These 2 rows form the pattern.

Judo-style dressing gown for toddlers

Wrap-over style dressing gowns are
popular for toddlers, especially as
the crossover fronts with tie belt help
it to fit more snugly for extra warmth.
The back and fronts have been knitted sideways to enable the stripes to
run vertically without the need for
making a double fabric by carrying
the yarn across the back of the work.

Sizes

To fit 56-61cm/22-24in chest loosely
Length to shoulder 55cm/21¾in
Sleeve seam 22cm/8¾in

You will need

3×50g balls of Sirdar Terry Look
 (90% acrylic, 10% nylon), in main
 colour A
2 balls each of 3 contrast colours, B,
 C and D
One pair 3mm/No 11 needles
One pair 3¼mm/No 10 needles

Tension

26 sts and 38 rows to 10cm/4in over
st st worked on 3¼mm/No 10 needles

Back

With 3¼mm/No 10 needles and A, cast
on 150 sts and beg at side seam. Beg
with a K row work 6 rows st st.
Next row K7 A, join in B, K143 B.
Next row P143 B, P7 A.
Rep last 2 rows 4 times more.
Keeping 7 sts at right-hand edge in
A throughout for hem at lower
edge, work 10 rows each in C, D
and A. **. Cont working 10 rows
each in B, C, D, A, D, C, B, A, D, C,
B and 6 rows A. Cast off.

Right front

Work as given for back to **
Shape front edge
Next row K7 A, K in B to last 3 sts,
K2 tog, K1.
Next row Using B, P1, P2 tog, P to
last 7 sts, P7 A.
Rep last 2 rows once more, then K
one row without shaping.
Cont dec in this way, working dec
on 4 rows then one row without
shaping, *at the same time* work 5
more rows in B, then 10 rows each in
C, D, A, B, C and D. 94 sts. Cast off.

Left front

Work first 6 rows as given for back.
Next row K in B to last 7 sts, K7 A.
Reversing position of hem as set,
work as given for right front,
working shaping at opposite end to
hem.

Sleeves

With 3mm/No 11 needles and A cast
on 70 sts. Beg with a K row work 10
rows in st st.
Change to 3¼mm/No 10 needles.
Cont in st st working 10 rows each
in A, B, C, D, A, B, C, D and 6 rows
A. Cast off.

Front band

With 3mm/No 11 needles and A cast
on 15 sts. Beg with a K row work in
st st until band is long enough to go
up front, round back neck and
down other front. Cast off.

Ties (make 2)

With 3mm/No 11 needles and A, cast
on 14 st and work in double st st as
foll:
1st row *K1, yfwd, sl 1, ybk, rep
from * to end.
Rep this row for 65cm/25½in or

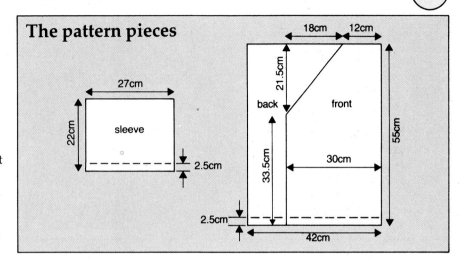

The pattern pieces

length required. Cast off K2 tog
along the row.

To make up

Do not press. Join shoulder seams.
Set in sleeves. Join side and sleeve
seams, leaving an opening in right
seam for tie to go through for a girl,
or left seam for a boy. Turn up hem
at lower edge and sl st in place.
Turn up hem of 10 rows on sleeve
and sl st in place. Sew on front
band, fold in half to inside and sl st
in place. Sew on ties.

Mosaic patterns in two or more colours

These sophisticated coloured patterns in combinations of horizontal stripes and slipped stitches could not be easier, but they have tremendous impact. Some look best in only two colours, others in as many colours as you wish.

Mosaic patterns can be used to create a wonderful variety of coloured fabrics, so don't be put off by their apparent intricacy – they are easy to work. Only one colour is used in any row, some of the stitches being knitted and others simply slipped from one needle to the other. Two rows are worked with the first colour. Then the next two rows are worked with a second colour – again, some of the stitches being knitted and others slipped, but in a different sequence.

Altering the sequence of knitted and slipped stitches causes parts of each pair of rows to be concealed by slipped stitches in a different colour carried up from the previous row. This way the slipped stitches form a superimposed pattern.

You can use only two colours throughout or introduce more colours in the following rows. In printed patterns the colours are coded as A, B, C and so on, for ease of reference and to allow you to substitute colours of your own choice, if you wish. If you are creating your own mosaic design, it is well worth coding your colours in this way so that you have a handy record of the sequence worked.

Purl or plain All mosaic patterns can be worked in either stocking stitch or garter stitch. If the instructions are for garter stitch and you want to work stocking stitch, simply purl all the wrong-side rows instead of knitting them. To work garter stitch instead of stocking stitch, knit the wrong side rows instead of purling them. If you are using a printed pattern, you may find it helpful to write in these adjustments, to save confusion.

The type of yarn you choose should relate to the effect you wish to achieve. The smooth surface of stocking stitch is complemented by bouclé or fluffy yarns, while the knobbly texture of garter stitch looks best worked in a plain yarn. Both fabrics look stunning when a glitter yarn is introduced as one of the colours.

Because stitches are slipped on every row the fabric is very dense.

Stitch requirements The fascinating thing about mosaics is that they can be worked over any number of stitches, so you are not tied to exact multiples of stitches.

Each example given here has an exact multiple of stitches shown but don't let this put you off if you want to experiment. Simply begin each right-side pattern row at the right-hand edge, as given, and work across the row until you run out of stitches, irrespective of what point you have reached in the pattern. Work the return row by knitting (or purling) all the knitted stitches of the previous row and slipping all the slipped stitches. The ends of the rows may not match exactly but these patterns are easy to incorporate into a basic design whether for a garment or household items such as bedcovers or cushion covers.

The easiest mosaic pattern to practise if you are a beginner is the tricolour pattern as this has a pattern repeat of only four rows with the effect being formed by changes in the colour of the yarn.

Working mosaic patterns

The right side rows are always knitted. Every slipped stitch is slipped with the yarn at the *back* on right-side rows and the same stitch is slipped again with the yarn at the *front* on following wrong side rows. The colours are alternated after every two rows and each slipped stitch – spanning two rows – is caught in again with its own, or an additional colour, on the third row. To begin, cast on with colour A and work the number of rows given.

Knitting a right side row
Join in B. Keep the yarn at the *back* of the work, *K the number of stitches given, slip the number of stitches given in a purlwise direction, repeat from * to end.

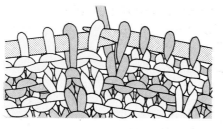

Knitting a wrong side row
Using same colour as previous row, keep the yarn at the back and knit all knitted stitches and bring the yarn forward to the front to slip all slipped stitches of the previous row.

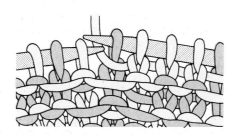

Purling a wrong side row
Using same colour as for previous row, keep the yarn at the front and purl all the knitted stitches and slip all the slipped stitches of the previous row.

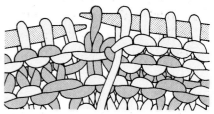

Turret pattern

Using A cast on multiples of 4 sts plus 3, eg 23.
1st row (Rs) Using A, K to end.
2nd row Using A, P to end.
3rd row Using B, K3, *sl 1, K3, rep from * to end.

4th row Using B, K3, *yfwd, sl 1, ybk, K3, rep from * to end.
5th row Using A, K2, *sl 1, K1, rep from * to last st, K1.
6th row Using A, P2, *sl 1, P1, rep from * to last st, P1.
7th row Using B, K1, *sl 1, K3, rep from * to last 2 sts, sl 1, K1.
8th row Using B, K1, *yfwd, sl 1, ybk, K3, rep from * to last 2 sts, yfwd, sl 1, ybk, K1.
9th and 10th rows Using A, as 1st and 2nd.
11th and 12th rows Using B, as 7th and 8th.
13th and 14th rows Using A, as 5th and 6th.

15th and 16th rows Using B, as 3rd and 4th.
These 16 rows form the pattern. To work in more than two colours use different colours for next repeat.

Tricolour pattern

Using A cast on multiples of 4 sts plus 3, eg 23.
1st row (Rs) Using A, *K3, sl 1, rep from * to last 3 sts, K3.
2nd row Using A, K3, *yfwd, sl 1, ybk, K3, rep from * to end.
3rd row Using B, K1, *sl 1, K3, rep from * to last 2 sts, sl 1, K1.
4th row Using B, K1, *yfwd, sl 1, ybk, K3, rep from * to last 2 sts, yfwd, sl 1, ybk, K1.
5th and 6th rows Using C, as 1st and 2nd.
7th and 8th rows Using A, as 3rd and 4th.
9th and 10th rows Using B, as 1st and 2nd.

11th and 12th rows Using C, as 3rd and 4th.
These 12 rows form the pattern. To work in two colours only repeat first 4 rows.

Overcheck pattern

Using A cast on multiples of 6 sts, eg 24. P one row.
1st row (Rs) Using B, K5, *sl 2, K4, rep from * to last st K1.
2nd row Using B, K5, *yfwd, sl 2, ybk, K4, rep from * to last st, K1.
3rd row Using A, K1, *sl 1, K2, rep from * to last 2 sts, sl 1, K1.
4th row Using A, P1, *sl 1, P2, rep from * to last 2 sts, sl 1, P1.
5th row Using B, K2, *sl 2, K4, rep from * to last 4 sts, sl 2, K2.
6th row Using B, K2, *yfwd, sl 2, ybk, K4, rep from * to last 4 sts, yfwd, sl 2, ybk, K2.
7th and 8th rows Using A, as 3rd and 4th.
These 8 rows form the pattern. This pattern is best worked in two colours only.

Greek key pattern

Using A cast on multiples of 6 sts plus 2, eg 26.
1st row (Rs) Using A, K to end.
2nd row Using A, K to end.
3rd row Using B, K1, *sl 1, K5, rep from * to last st, K1.
4th and every alt row Using same colour as previous row keep yarn at front of work to sl all sl sts of previous row and take it back to K all K sts.
5th row Using A, K2, *sl 1, K3, sl 1, K1, rep from * to end.
7th row Using B, K1, *sl 1, K3, sl 1, K1, rep from * to last st, K1.

9th row Using A, K6, *sl 1, K5, rep from * to last 2 sts, sl 1, K1.

11th and 12th rows Using B, as 1st and 2nd.

13th row Using A, K4, *sl 1, K5, rep from * to last 4 sts, sl 1, K3.

15th row Using B, *K3, sl 1, K1, sl 1, rep from * to last 2 sts, K2.

17th row Using A, K2, *sl 1, K1, sl 1, K3, rep from * to end.

19th row Using B, K3, *sl 1, K5, rep from * to last 5 sts, sl 1, K4.

20th row As 4th.

These 20 rows form the pattern. To work in more than two colours use different colours for next repeat.

Pyramid pattern

Using A cast on multiples of 14 sts plus 3, eg 31. K one row.

1st row (Rs) Using B, K8, *sl 1, K13, rep from * to last 9 sts, sl 1, K8.

2nd and every alt row Using same colour as previous row keep yarn at front of work to sl all sl sts of previous row and take it back to K all K sts.

3rd row Using A, K2, *(sl 1, K1) twice, sl 1, K3, (sl 1, K1) 3 times, rep from * to last st, K1.

5th row Using B, K7, *sl 1, K1, sl 1, K11, rep from * to last 10 sts, sl 1, K1, sl 1, K7.

7th row Using A, K2, *sl 1, K1, sl 1, K7, (sl 1, K1) twice, rep from * to last st, K1.

9th row Using B, K5, *(sl 1, K1) 3 times, sl 1, K7, rep from * to last 12 sts, (sl 1, K1) 3 times, sl 1, K5.

11th row Using A, K2, *sl 1, K11, sl 1, K1, rep from * to last st, K1.

13th row Using B, K3, *(sl 1, K1) 5 times, sl 1, K3, rep from * to end.

15th row Using A, K1, *sl 1, K13, rep from * to last 2 sts, sl 1, K1.

16th row As 2nd.

These 16 rows form the pattern. To work in more than two colours use different colours for next repeat.

More multi-coloured patterns

In jacquard knitting a single, multi-coloured motif or repeats of the motif forming a pattern are used to highlight basic garments. Random pictorial and regular geometric collage patterns produce all-over fabrics. These techniques use many colours in any one row.

Jacquard, random pictorial and regular geometric collage patterns (also called intarsia knitting), use any number of colours in the same row and are worked in stocking stitch.

It is possible to work a small jacquard design using only three colours in any row, by stranding the yarns across the back of the fabric. To strand more than three colours makes the fabric clumsy and untidy. In a random pictorial pattern small areas may have the yarn stranded or woven in across the back, while larger areas need to be worked with separate balls of colour. In consequence some areas of the fabric will be of double thickness and others of single thickness so it is particularly important to keep the tension regular and even – otherwise you will emphasize the irregularities already inherent in the design.

The correct method for working all large jacquard motifs, all-over-pictorial or geometric collage patterns and wide vertical stripes is to use small, separate balls of yarn for each colour. As each new colour is brought into use loop it round the previous one to avoid leaving a gap in the fabric. Work with short lengths of each contrast colour or the yarns will become very tangled and difficult to unravel.

An alternative is to use bobbins – see Professional Touch overleaf. These patterns form fabrics of single thickness as the yarns are not stranded across the back of the work.

Joining in new colours

On jacquard and pictorial patterns when more than four stitches have to be worked in one colour, weave in the yarn on every alternate stitch. This avoids long, loose strands of yarn on the back of the fabric which catch and snag in wear.

On wide vertical stripes and regular geometric collage patterns, loop each new colour round the last stitch in the previous colour on every row. If you do not, you will produce unjoined stripes or shapes of each colour.

On large motifs and random pictorial patterns, loop the new colour yarn round the last stitch in the previous yarn in any row where the same number of stitches have been worked in one colour, to avoid a gap in the fabric. With such patterns and motifs, however, some stitches will inevitably overlap other areas of colour – in which event the yarn will automatically be looped and the fabric closed.

Weaving in yarns across the fabric

Working a knit row

Keep the yarns at the back of the work throughout and repeat the following action each time a new colour is brought into use.
1 Knit the first stitch with the first colour in the right hand.

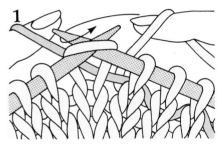

2 On the second and every following *alternate* stitch in the first colour, insert the right-hand needle from front to back into the stitch. Use the left hand to place the contrast yarn not being used over the top of the right-hand needle, then knit the stitch with the first colour. The stitches in between are knitted in the usual way.

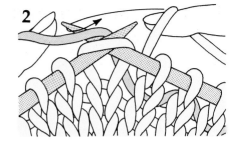

Working a purl row

Keep the yarns at the front of the work throughout, and repeat the

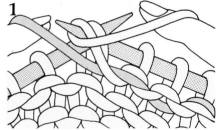

following action each time a new colour is brought into use.
1 To alternate the position of the weaving, purl the first two stitches with the first colour in the right hand.
2 On the third and every following *alternate* stitch in the first colour,

insert the right-hand needle from right to left into the stitch. Use the left hand to place the contrast yarn not in use across the top of the right-hand needle, then purl the stitch with the first colour. The stitches in between are purled in the usual way.

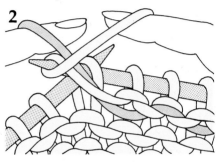

Changing colours in wide vertical stripes

Working a knit row

Keep the yarns at the back of the work throughout and repeat the following for each new colour.
Knit across the stitches in the first colour. Take this end of yarn over the top of the next colour to be used and drop it. Pick up the next colour

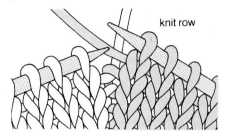

knit row

under this strand of yarn and take it over the strand ready to knit the next stitch.

Working a purl row

Keep the yarns at the front of the work throughout and repeat the following for each new colour.

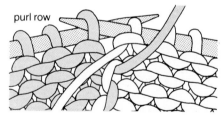

purl row

Purl across the stitches in the first colour. Take this end of yarn over the top of the next colour to be used and drop it. Pick up the next colour under this strand of yarn and take it over the strand ready to purl the next stitch.

Working jacquard patterns from charts

Jacquard motifs or repeating patterns use more than two colours in a row. Working from charts, the first and odd-numbered rows read from right to left and the second and even-numbered rows from left to right.

Chart for border pattern

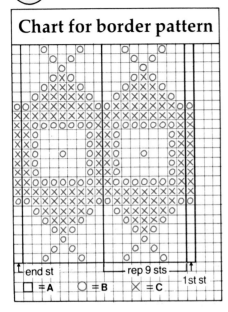

end st · · · · · · · · rep 9 sts · · · · · · · · 1st st

□ ≡ A   ○ ≡ B   ✕ ≡ C

Chart for rose pattern

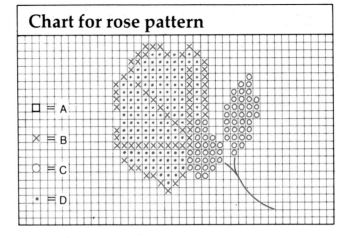

□ ≡ A

✕ ≡ B

○ ≡ C

• ≡ D

Right: A sample showing a rose motif in double knitting yarn. Embroider the stem afterwards in stem stitch.

Baby-size jerseys in hexagons and stripes

This pattern is very simple, with no shaping at all – a very good one on which to start collage knitting. Each jersey sports six colours in every row, so wind the yarns on to bobbins first to avoid getting into a tangle when changing colours.

If you cannot decide between the hexagons and the stripes, why not treat baby and knit them both.

Sizes

To fit 46cm/18in chest
Length to shoulder, 28cm/11in
Sleeve seam, 19cm/7½in

You will need

Striped jersey 1×50g ball of Robin Columbine Double Knitting (60% acrylic, 40% nylon) in main colour A
1 ball of same in each of 6 contrast colours B, C, D, E, F and G
Hexagon jersey 1×50g ball of Robin Columbine Double Knitting (60% acrylic, 40% nylon) in main colour A
1 ball of same in each of 6 contrast colours B, C, D, E, F and G
One pair 3mm/No 11 needles
One pair 3¾mm/No 9 needles
Four buttons

Tension

24 sts and 32 rows to 10cm/4in over st st worked on 3¾mm/No 9 needles

Striped jersey front

With 3mm/No 11 needles and A cast on 62 sts.
1st row (Rs) K2, *P2, K2, rep from * to end.
2nd row P2, *K2, P2, rep from * to end.
Rep these 2 rows 5 times more. Break off A.**
Change to 3¾mm/No 9 needles. Beg with a K row cont in st st and vertical stripes as foll, twisting colours where they join on every row:
Next row K11 B, 10 C, 10 D, 10 E, 10 F, 11 G.
Next row P11 G, 10 F, 10 E, 10 D, 10 C, 11 B.
Rep these 2 rows until work measures 26cm/10¼in from beg, ending with a Ws row. Break off

contrast colours. Join in A. K one row.
Beg with a 2nd row work 5 rows rib as given for welt.
***Next row** (buttonhole row) (K2, P2, K2, P2 tog, yon) twice, rib to last 16 sts, (yrn, P2 tog, K2, P2, K2) twice.
Work 2 more rows in rib. Cast off in rib.

Striped jersey back

Work as given for front, omitting buttonholes.

Striped jersey sleeves

With 3mm/No 11 needles and A cast on 30 sts. Work 11 rows rib as given for back.
Next row (inc row) Rib 4, *pick up loop lying between needles and K tbl – **called M1**, rib 2, rep from * 10 times more, M1, rib 4. 42 sts.
Break off A.****
Change to 3¾mm/No 9 needles. Beg with a K row cont in st st and vertical stripes as foll, twisting colours where they join on every row:

Next row K11 B, 10 C, 10 D, 11 E.
Next row P11 E, 10 D, 10 C, 11 B.
Rep these 2 rows until sleeve
measures 19cm/7½in from beg,
ending with a Ws row. Cast off
loosely.

Hexagon jersey front

Work as given for striped jersey
front to **.
Change to 3¾mm/No 9 needles.
Beg with a K row cont in st st and
hexagon patt as foll, using separate
small balls of each colour and
twisting colours where they join on
every row:
1st row K11 B, 10 C, 10 D, 10 E, 10 F
11 G.
Beg with a P row work 3 rows st st
in colours as now set.
5th row K2 E, 8 B, 2 F, 8 C, 2 G, 8 D,
2 B, 8 E, 2 C, 8 F, 2 D, 8 G, 2 E.
Cont in this way working in patt
from chart until 72 rows have been
completed. Break off contrast colours.
Join in A. K one row. Complete as
given for striped jersey front from
*** to end.

Hexagon jersey back

Work as given for front, omitting
buttonholes

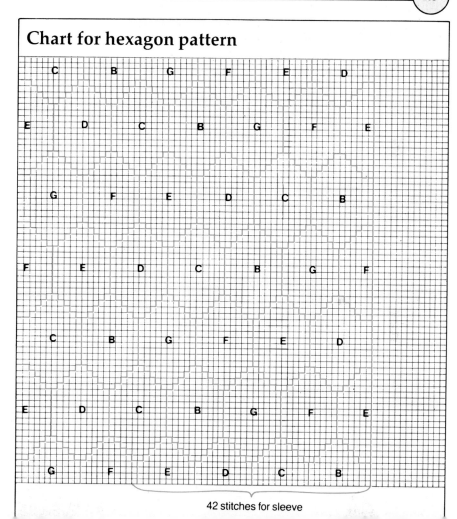

Chart for hexagon pattern

42 stitches for sleeve

Hexagon jersey sleeves

Work as given for striped jersey sleeves to ****.
Change to 3¾mm/No 9 needles.
Beg with a K row cont in st st,

working in patt as given on chart until 48 rows have been completed. Cast off loosely.

To make up
Press each piece under a dry cloth with a warm iron.

Both versions Lap front shoulder over back and st down at armhole edge. Sew in sleeves. Join side and sleeve seams. Sew on buttons.

_____ PROFESSIONAL TOUCH _____

Knitting with bobbins

Small bobbins can be used to keep the various colours free of tangles. Wind each colour round a separate bobbin. As each one needs to be brought into use it hangs ready at the back of the work and tangle-free.
1 To make a bobbin, simply cut the shape from stiff cardboard, making a narrow opening at the top of each, as shown, to allow the yarn to unravel. Cut one bobbin for each colour used.

2 Wind a small amount of yarn round the bobbin, passing the working end of the yarn through the slit.
As each new colour is required, join it in with a slip loop. Work the number of stitches with each colour after first twisting it round the last stitch in the previous colour. When a colour is not in use, leave the bobbin hanging at the back of the work in readiness for when it is required again.

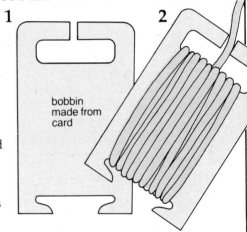

1

2

bobbin made from card

Timeless and true Fair Isle

Fair Isle is the original multi-coloured, patterned knitting from the Shetland Island of that name. There are many pale imitations, but it is the colour sequence that sets the true Fair Isle in a class on its own. Knit a tam-o-shanter and judge for yourself.

Authentic Fair Isle patterns are Spanish in origin, probably introduced to the island by shipwrecked sailors of the Armada.

The original Fair Isle knitters worked all their garments in the round. This is an ideal method for coloured knitting because the front of the knitting is always facing you and all rounds are knitted. When the knitting had to be divided, as at the underarm, the yarns were broken off at the end of each row and rejoined at the beginning of the next. Flat knitting can also be used for these patterns which are always worked in stocking stitch.

Fair Isle designs are different from other coloured knitting in the particular way that the colours are changed on every row.

The number of stitches worked in any colour is never so great that the yarn cannot easily be stranded across the back of the fabric.

In a traditional pattern sequence, a broad band is worked in a number of colours followed by a narrow band worked in just two or three colours. The backgrounds are in natural colours – cream, beige or grey – to set off the strong, bright colours in the designs.

To achieve a different look, while using the same patterns, the colour emphasis can be reversed so that the bright colours form the background and the natural shades the design. The main aim is to keep the level of contrast between the background and the design constant.

No more than two colours at a time are used in a row, a method that produces an even fabric of double thickness as the yarns are carried across the back of the work when not being used. The multi-coloured effect is achieved simply by changing the background colour on one row and the contrast colour on the next row, continuing this sequence throughout all the patterns.

Abstract or pictorial

In an abstract design the sequence is two rows in each background colour and two rows in each contrast colour to the centre of the chart. The centre row is worked in the main colours chosen for the design, to emphasize them, then the original colours and pattern rows are reversed back down the chart to the beginning again. Pictorial designs carry on altering the colour sequence to the end of the chart.

Here is just one colour sequence used for a narrow band of pattern in four colours.

1st row Background A, pattern B.
2nd row Background A, pattern C.
3rd row Background D, pattern C.
4th row As 1st.
5th row As 3rd.
6th row As 2nd.
7th row As 1st.
Fair Isle patterns can be knitted simultaneously with both hands. The right hand is used throughout to knit with one colour and the left hand to knit with the other. This may be complicated at first glance but once you have tried it and discovered how simple it is, knitting coloured patterns in any other way will seem strange.

Reading a Fair Isle chart

Reading a Fair Isle chart is by no means as daunting as you might suppose. Each square represents one stitch horizontally and one row vertically. The chart shows the multiples of stitches needed for each pattern repeat, plus any edge stitches required to make the pattern match at side seams.

Each colour is coded with a different letter in the instructions, the first colour used as A, the second as B and so on. Each of these letters is represented by a symbol on the chart.

In flat knitting

Right side rows are knitted and wrong side rows are purled.

Begin the first row at the lower right-hand corner of the chart and knit across the row, working any edge stitches shown only at the beginning and end of the row and repeating the multiples of stitches across the row. Begin the second row at the left-hand side of the chart and purl across the row to the end, working the edge stitches as before.

Alternate the rows from right to left on the knit rows and from left to right on the purl rows.

In circular knitting

All the rounds are knitted and the right side of the work is always facing you.

Begin each round at the right-hand edge of the chart and work across to the left-hand edge. Only the multiples of stitches needed for each pattern repeat are worked and any edge stitches are omitted, as in the charts for the tam-o-shanter.

Chart A

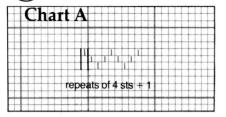

repeats of 4 sts + 1

□ = A natural

| = contrast colour

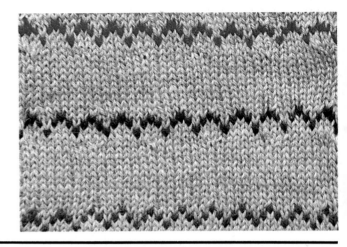

Chart B

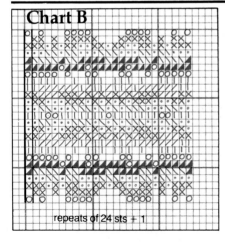

repeats of 24 sts + 1

□ = A natural
• = C yellow
✕ = B brown
○ = D blue
＼ = F red
▲ = G camel
| = H green
／ = E cream

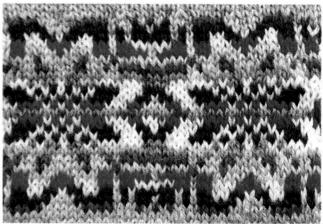

Chart C

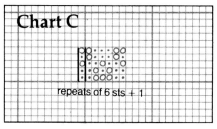

repeats of 6 sts + 1

• = C yellow
O = D blue

Chart D

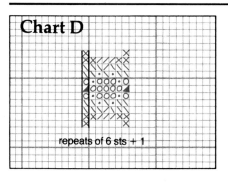

repeats of 6 sts + 1

□ = A natural
✕ = B brown
\ = F red
/ = E cream
• = C yellow
O = D blue
◤ = G camel

Traditional tam-o-shanter

Robert Burns' famous character, Tam o'Shanter, gives his name to the type of beret known as a tammy. The ribbed headband is in the main background colour and the bands of coloured patterns are introduced as you increase stitches towards the widest part. Then the stitches are gradually decreased again to form the crown. You can knit yourself a jaunty tam-o-shanter while trying out one of these lovely traditional Fair Isle patterns. If you want a different pattern from the one illustrated, you could use one of the other charts for the first 32 rounds, filling in with plain rounds if necessary.

Size

Diameter at widest point about 27cm/10¾in
To fit an average adult head

You will need

1×50g ball of Patons Clansman 4 ply (100% wool) in main colour A
1 ball each of same in contrast colours, B, C, D, E, F and G
Set of four 2¾mm/No 12 needles
Set of four 3¼mm/ No 10 needles

Tension

28 st and 36 rows to 10cm/4in over st st and 32 st and 32 rows to 10cm/4in over Fair Isle patt worked on 3¼mm/No 10 needles

Note

To work tam-o-shanter from charts E and F read all rounds from right to left.

Tam-o-shanter

With set of four 2¾mm/No 12 needles and A cast on 144 sts, 48 on each of 3 needles. Work 10 rounds K1, P1 rib.
Next round (inc round) *Rib 2 sts, pick up loop lying between sts and K tbl, rep from * to end. 216 sts. Change to set of four 3¼mm/No 10 needles. K 3 rounds st st. Commence Fair Isle patt. Join in and break off colours as required. Work in patt from Chart E , rep the 6 patt sts 36 times, until 16 rounds have been completed. Rep these 16 rounds once more.

Shape crown

Next round Using A, *K2 tog, K4, rep from * to end. 180 sts.

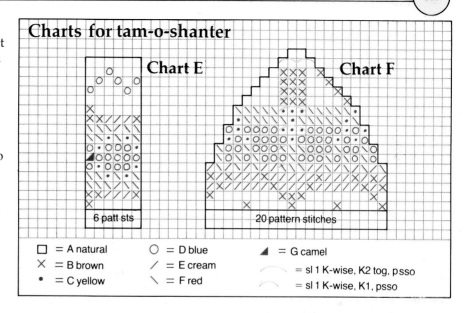

Charts for tam-o-shanter

Chart E

Chart F

6 patt sts

20 pattern stitches

☐ = A natural   ○ = D blue   ◢ = G camel

✕ = B brown   ╱ = E cream

• = C yellow   ╲ = F red

⌢ = sl 1 K-wise, K2 tog, p sso

⌢ = sl 1 K-wise, K1, psso

Next round Using A, K to end.

Next round Using A, *K2 tog, K7, rep from * to end. 160 sts. Commence Fair Isle patt. Join in and break off colours as required. Work in patt from Chart F, rep the 20 patt sts 8 times, then dec as indicated on 5th, 7th, 9th, 11th, 12th, 13th, 14th, 15th and 16th rounds, until 16 sts rem.

Break off yarn, thread through rem sts, draw up tightly and fasten off securely.

To make up

Tam-o-shanter requires pressing only. Cut a circle of card 27cm/ 10¾in in diameter. Insert into tammy and press lightly under a damp cloth with a warm iron, omitting ribbing.

Lace knitting for beautiful backgrounds

Lace knitting has such a variety of patterns that most beginners are bewildered by the profusion and assume the working methods are complicated. In fact, many small lace patterns are quicker and more interesting to knit than most textured patterns, such as guernseys.

All lace patterns are built up with a sequence of eyelet hole increases, using the yarn forward, over the needle or round the needle methods, see pages 30-34. Stitches must then be decreased in the course of the pattern to compensate for the eyelet increases. The decreases are worked by the normal methods given on pages 36-40. The decreases will not necessarily immediately precede or follow the eyelet increases. In fact, it is the way in which the eyelets are grouped that gives lace knitting its incredible variety – the permutations are almost limitless.

Lace knitting provides for every degree of skill – only a very few patterns are really complicated. To simplify your first attempt, work two vertical panels on the front of a basic stocking stitch jersey, placing them well away from any edges where shaping will take place.

It takes a little practice to tackle shaping in an all-over lace pattern. It is not too difficult if you remember that when decreasing, every time an eyelet hole increase is eliminated from the pattern sequence its corresponding decrease must also be eliminated. Similarly, when increasing, remember that you must not work a new eyelet increase in the pattern sequence until you have also added sufficient stitches to work its corresponding decrease.

Multiples of stitches in knitting patterns

Stocking stitch and garter stitch are worked over any number of stitches, but even single rib needs multiples of two stitches plus one at the edge if seams are to match exactly. More complicated patterns need larger multiples of stitches. When creating a pattern, the designer must take this into account to ensure that the pattern repeats work out accurately. Sometimes extra stitches are needed at each end of the row so that patterns match up correctly when joined.

The simple lace patterns illustrated below repeat over six stitches. This means that the number of stitches cast on must be a multiple of six, plus one edge stitch. So to begin, you need to cast on a minimum of seven stitches, adding six more for each pattern repeat – 13, 19, 25 and so on. Instructions for the edge stitches are

given at the beginning and end of each row. The multiples of six stitches needed for the pattern are given after the asterisk, *, and are repeated as instructed.

Sample worked in mesh lace.

Sample worked in catkin lace.

Mesh lace
1st row K1, *yfwd, sl 1, K1, psso, K1, K2 tog, yfwd, K1, rep from * to end.
2nd and every alt row P to end.

Sample worked in arrowhead lace.

Sample worked in miniature leaf lace.

3rd row K1, *yfwd, K1, sl 1, K2 tog, psso, K1, yfwd, K1, rep from * to end.
5th row K1, *K2 tog, yfwd, K1, yfwd, sl 1, K1, psso, K1, rep from * to end.
7th row K2 tog, *(K1, yfwd) twice, K1, sl 1, K2 tog, psso, rep from * to last 5 sts, (K1, yfwd) twice, K1, sl 1, K1, psso.
8th row As 2nd.
These 8 rows form the pattern.

Arrowhead lace
1st row K1, *K2 tog, yfwd, K1, yfwd, sl 1, K1, psso, K1, rep from * to end.
2nd and every alt row P to end.
3rd row K2 tog, *yfwd, K3, yfwd, sl 1, K2 tog, psso, rep from * to last 5 sts, yfwd, K3, yfwd, sl 1, K1, psso.
5th row K1, *yfwd, sl 1, K1, psso, K1, K2 tog, yfwd, K1, rep from * to end.
7th row As 5th.
9th row As 5th.
11th row K2, *yfwd, sl 1, K2 tog, psso, yfwd, K3, rep from * to last 5 sts, yfwd, sl 1, K2 tog, psso, yfwd, K2.

12th row As 2nd.
These 12 rows form the pattern.

Catkin lace

1st row K3, *yfwd, sl 1, K1, psso, K4, rep from * to last 4 sts, yfwd, sl 1, K1, psso, K2.
2nd and every alt row P to end.
3rd row K1, *K2 tog, yfwd, K1, yfwd, sl 1, K1, psso, K1, rep from * to end.
5th row K2 tog, yfwd, *K3, yfwd, sl 1, K2 tog, psso, yfwd, rep from * to last 5 sts, K3, yfwd, sl 1, K1, psso.
7th row K1, *yfwd, sl 1, K1, psso, K1, K2 tog, yfwd, K1, rep from * to end.
9th row As 7th.
10th row As 2nd.
These 10 rows form the pattern.

Miniature leaf lace

1st row K1, *K2 tog, yfwd, K1, yfwd, sl 1, K1, psso, K1, rep from * to end.
2nd and every alt row P to end.
3rd row Sl 1, K1, psso, *yfwd, K3, yfwd, sl 2 tog in knitwise direction, K1, p2sso, rep from * to last 5 sts, yfwd, K3, yfwd, K2 tog.
5th row K1, *yfwd, sl 1, K1, psso,

K1, K2 tog, yfwd, K1, rep from * to end.
7th row K2, *yfwd, sl 2, K1, p2sso, yfwd, K3, rep from * to last 5 sts, yfwd, sl 2, K1, p2sso, yfwd, K2.
8th row As 2nd.
These 8 rows form the pattern.

You can make a most attractive cot or pram cover using squares of all of the lace samples that have multiples of the same number of stitches, and mixing there with squares of basic patterns, such as stocking, garter and moss stitches.
Add a lace border using one of the patterns given on pages 116-121. These edgings are knitted sideways across a short pattern row so you can easily calculate the yarn needed and the length to knit.

Cot or pram cover made from lace squares

Calculate the multiples of stitches needed to give the size of square

you require. As a guide, the lace stitches that have multiples of 10 stitches plus one stitch, worked in double knitting yarn on 4mm/No 8 needles over 21 stitches will give a square about 9–10cm/3½–4in. Use up oddments of the same yarn in different colours or keep to one colour only for all of the squares. See how many squares you can make out of one ball of yarn to arrive at the total quantity you will need. Allow sufficient to make a lace edging to complete the cover. The lace patterns are not reversible, so sew all the squares together so that the seams are on the wrong side, then press them lightly as given on the ball band.
Choose the edging you like best and pin it into place around the outer edges as you knit it. Once you are sure you have sufficient length, cast off and join the two short edges together. Keep this seam at one corner of the centre squares and sew the edging into place. Press the seams as before.

ruffle edging

Queen's lace edging

pleated lace
edging

Knitted lace for collars and edgings

Knitted lace edgings add a touch of luxury to home items and clothes — learn how to knit them in with the neckband of a garment.

Our great-grandmothers had a passion for decorating everything with knitted or crocheted lace. Rediscover this inexpensive way of adding a touch of individuality to a favourite ready-made or hand-knitted garment.

Knit them in fine cotton to make fresh and dainty trimmings for household linens.

Use a fine acrylic yarn to make beautiful soft edgings for baby garments, or a lightweight chunky yarn to give a decorative finish to plain shawls and baby blankets.

It is easy to calculate the total amount of yarn you will need, even on something as large as a tablecloth, by measuring how much you have worked using the first ball and use this to calculate how much more yarn you will need to complete the length required.

Ruffle edging is perfect for a beginner. It forms a firm, purled outer edging with a little border of garter stitch at the inside edge. The fluted effect is achieved by turning the work in the middle of some of the rows without knitting to the end, thus making the inside edge shorter than the outside edge. Use this lace round the edges of a chunky baby blanket.

Pleated lace is also suitable for a beginner. It has an eyelet hole and garter stitch border at the inside edge and a row of eyelets in the centre of each pleat. The pleats are achieved by turning the work in the middle of some of the rows, as for ruffle edge, giving a chevron effect to the lower edge. Use this as a hem on a baby dress and thread narrow ribbon through the border eyelets for additional decoration.

Garter stitch lace is another easy pattern. It has an eyelet hole and garter stitch border at the inside edge and eyelet holes are used to increase the stitches on the main pattern. These extra stitches are cast off at the end of each repeat of the pattern rows, forming a zigzag edge. This pattern forms a decorative little collar on a child's jersey as shown in this chapter.

Ruffle edging

Cast on 13 sts.
1st row (Rs) K.
2nd row P10 sts, turn and K these 10 sts.
3rd row P10 sts, K3.
4th row K3, P10 sts.
5th row K10 sts, turn and P these 10 sts.
6th row K.
These 6 rows form the pattern.

Pleated lace edging

Cast on 16 sts.
1st row (Ws) P.
2nd row K1, sl 1, K1, psso, yfwd and round needle twice to make 2 loops – **called yrn twice**, K2 tog, P8, inc in next st, K2.
3rd row K14, P1, K2
4th row K1, sl 1, K1, psso, yrn twice, K2 tog, P9, inc in next st, K2.
5th row K12, turn, P9, inc in next st, K2.
6th row K16, P1, K2.
7th row K1, sl 1, K1, psso, yrn

twice, K2 tog, P1, (yrn, P2 tog) 5 times, P1, K2.
8th row K13, turn, P9, P2 tog, K2.
9th row K15, P1, K2.
10th row K1, sl 1, K1, psso, yrn twice, K2 tog, P9, P2 tog, K2.
11th row As 3rd.
12th row K1, sl 1, K1, psso, yrn twice, K2 tog, P8, P2 tog, K2.
13th row K13, P1, K2.
14th row K1, sl 1, K1, psso, yrn twice, K2 tog, K11.
15th row K2, P8, turn and K10.
16th row As 15th.
17th row K2, P9, K2, P1, K2.
The 2nd to 17th rows inclusive form the pattern.

Garter stitch lace edging

Cast on 6 sts.
1st row (Rs) Yfwd and over needle to inc 1 – **called inc 1**, K2 tog, K2, yfwd, K2. 7 sts.
2nd row K5, yfwd, K2 tog.
3rd row Inc 1, K2 tog, K2, yfwd, K1, yfwd, K2.
4th row K7, yfwd, K2 tog.
5th row Inc 1, K2 tog, K2, (yfwd, K1) 3 times, yfwd, K2. 13 sts.
6th row Cast off 7 sts, K4 including st on needle, yfwd, K2 tog. 6 sts.
These 6 rows form the pattern.

Little girl's jersey with lacy collar

This jersey is worked in a pretty eyelet lace pattern with a garter stitch lace collar and neckband in a contrasting colour. The back, front and sleeves are shaped at the armhole into a semi-raglan and all joined into a yoke with back opening.

Sizes

To fit 56 [61:66]cm/22 [24:26]in chest
Length from back neck,
31 [34:37]cm/12¼ [13½:14½]in
Sleeve seam, 21 [23:25]cm/
8¼ [9:9¾]in
The figures in [] refer to the 61/24 and 66cm/26in sizes respectively

You will need

2 [2:3]×50g balls of Wendy Choice
  4 ply (65% Courtelle acrylic,
  20% wool, 15% Bri-nylon) in main
  colour A
1 [1:1] ball of same in contrast
  colour B
One pair 2¾mm/No 12 needles
One pair 3¼mm/No 10 needles
Set of four 3¼mm/No 10 needles
  pointed at both ends
Three buttons

Tension

28 sts and 36 rows to 10cm/4in over eyelet hole patt worked on 3¼mm/No 10 needles

Back

With 2¾mm/No 12 needles and A cast on 79 [87:95] sts.
1st row (Rs) K1, *P1, K1, rep from * to end.
2nd row P1, *K1, P1, rep from * to end.

Rep these 2 rows until work measures 4cm/1½in from beg, ending with a 2nd row and inc one st at end of last row. 80 [88:96] sts. Change to 3¼mm/No 10 needles. Commence eyelet hole patt.

1st row (Rs) K.
2nd and every alt row P.
3rd row K3, *yfwd, K2 tog, K6, rep from * to last 5 sts, yfwd, K2 tog, K3.
5th row K.
7th row K7, *yfwd, K2 tog, K6, rep from * to last st, K1.
8th row P.

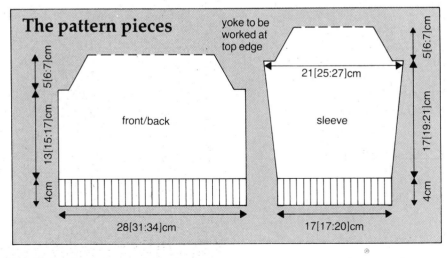

The pattern pieces

yoke to be worked at top edge

front/back
5[6:7]cm
13[15:17]cm
4cm
28[31:34]cm

sleeve
5[6:7]cm
21[25:27]cm
17[19:21]cm
4cm
17[17:20]cm

These 8 rows form the patt. Rep patt rows 5 [6:7] times more.

Shape armholes

Keeping patt correct throughout, cast off 3 sts at beg of next 2 rows.

3rd row K2 tog, *K6, yfwd, K2 tog, rep from * to last 8 sts, K6, K2 tog tbl.

4th and every alt row P.

5th row K2 tog, K to last 2 sts, K2 tog tbl.

7th row K2 tog, *yfwd, K2 tog, K6, rep from * to last 4 sts, yfwd, K2 tog, K2 tog tbl.

Keeping eyelet holes in line one above the other as now set cont dec in this way at each end of every alt row until 58 [62:66] sts rem, ending with a Ws row.

Next row K2 tog, K2 [4:6] sts, *yfwd, K2 tog, K6, rep from * to last 6 [8:10] sts, yfwd, K2 tog, K2 [4:6] sts, K2 tog tbl.

Next row P.

Next row K2 tog, K to last 2 sts, K2 tog tbl.

Next row P. 54 [58:62] sts.

3rd size only

Next row K2 tog, K4, *yfwd, K2 tog, K6, rep from * to last 8 sts, yfwd, K2 tog, K4, K2 tog tbl.
Next row P.
Next row K2 tog, K to last 2 sts, K2 tog tbl.
Next row P. 58 sts.

All sizes

Break off yarn. Leave sts on holder.

Front

Work as given for back.

Sleeves

With 2¾mm/No 12 needles and A cast on 47 [47:55] sts. Work 4cm/1½in rib as given for back, ending with a 2nd row and inc one st at end of last row. 48 [48:56] sts.
Change to 3¼mm/No 10 needles. Work first 8 patt rows as given for back.
Keeping patt correct throughout, inc one st at each end of next and every foll 8th [4th:6th] row until there are 60 [70:76] sts.
Cont without shaping until 15th [17th:19th] eyelet hole row has been worked from beg, ending with a Ws row.

Shape top

Keeping patt correct throughout, cast off 3 sts at beg of next 2 rows.
Dec one st at each end of next and every alt row until 38 [44:46] sts rem, ending with a Ws row.
Next row K2 tog, K4 [3:4] sts, *yfwd, K2 tog, K6, rep from * until 8 [7:8] sts rem, yfwd, K2 tog, K4 [3:4] sts, K2 tog tbl.
Next row P. 36 [42:44] sts.
Keeping eyelet holes in line one above the other as now set on every 4th row as now set, cont dec one st at each end of next and every alt row until 34 [40:38] sts rem, ending with a Ws row.
Break off yarn. Leave sts on holder.

Yoke

With Rs of back facing, set of four 3¼mm/No 10 needles and A, sl first 29 [31:31] sts on to a spare needle, rejoin yarn to rem sts on left-hand needle, cast on 4 sts for underflap button band at centre back, turn and cont working in rows.

1st size only

1st row K4 button band sts, K1, (K2 tog, K2, yfwd, K2 tog, K2) 3 times, work across first sleeve (K2 tog, K2, yfwd, K2 tog, K2) 4 times, K2 tog tbl, work across front sts (K2, yfwd, K2 tog, K2, K2 tog) 6 times, K2, yfwd, K2 tog, K2, work across 2nd sleeve (K2 tog, K2, yfwd, K2 tog, K2) 4 times, K2 tog tbl, work across right back (K2, yfwd, K2 tog, K2, K2 tog) 3 times, K5. 158 sts.

2nd size only

1st row K4 button band sts, K1, (K2 tog, K2, yfwd, K2 tog, K2) 3 times, K2 tog, work across first sleeve K2 tog, K1, (yfwd, K2 tog, K2, K2 tog, K2) 4 times, yfwd, K2 tog, K1, K2 tog, work across front sts (K2 tog, K2, yfwd, K2 tog, K2) 7 times, K2 tog, work across 2nd sleeve as for first sleeve, work across right back (K2 tog, K2, yfwd, K2 tog, K2) 3 times, K2 tog, K5. 172 sts.

3rd size only

1st row K4 button band sts, work across back sts as given for 2nd size, work across first sleeve (K2, yfwd, K2 tog, K2, K2 tog) 4 times, K2, yfwd, K2 tog, K2, work across front sts as given for 2nd size, work across 2nd sleeve as given for first sleeve, work across right back as given for 2nd size. 172 sts.

All sizes

2nd and every alt row K4, P to last 4 sts, K4.

3rd row K.

5th row (dec row) K4, *K2 tog, K2, yfwd, K2 tog, K1, rep from * to last 7 sts, K2 tog, K5. 135 [148:148] sts. Rep 2nd to 4th rows once.

9th row (dec and buttonhole row) K3, *K2 tog, K2, yfwd, K2 tog, rep from * to last 7 sts, K2 tog, K1, K2 tog, and yfwd for buttonhole, K2. 114 [124:124] sts.

Rep 2nd to 4th rows once.

13th row (dec row) K4, *K2 tog, yfwd, K2 tog, K1, rep from * to last 5 sts, K2 tog, K3. 92 [100:100] sts.

Rep 2nd to 4th rows once.

17th row (dec row) K5, *yfwd, (K2 tog) twice, yfwd, K2 tog, K2, rep from * 9 [10:10] times more, yfwd, K2 tog, K to end. 82 [89:89] sts.

Beg with a P row work 5 rows st st with g st borders, working buttonhole as before on 2nd row. Leave sts on holder.

Lace collar

With 3¼mm/No 10 needles and B cast on 6 sts. Work 6 rows patt as given for g st lace edging. Rep patt rows until 24 [26:26] patt have been completed. K one row. Cast off. With Rs of inside edge facing and 3¼mm/No 10 needles, pick up and K74 [81:81] sts along straight edge. P one row. Leave sts for time being.

Neckband

With Rs of work facing, 2¼mm/No 12 needles and A, K4 sts of underflap, drop A and pick up B, with needle holding collar sts in front of needle holding neckband sts, *K1 st from collar and neckband tog, rep from * to last 4 sts, using small separate ball of A, K4 sts of button band. 82 [89:89] sts.

Next row K4 A, using B, P to last 4 sts, dec one st in centre on 1st size only, K4 A. 81 [89:89] sts.

Next row K4 A, using B, work in K1, P1 rib to last 5 sts, K1, K4 A.

Next row K4 A, using B, work in P1, K1 rib to last 5 sts, P1, K4 A.

Rep last 2 rows once more.

Next row (buttonhole row) K4 A, using B rib to last 4 sts, using A K2 tog, yfwd, K2.

Work 2 more rows as now set. Cast off.

To make up

Press each piece lightly under a dry cloth with a cool iron. Join underarm seams on sleeves. Join side seams. Sew down lower end of button band to back. Press seams. Sew on buttons. Catch down ends of lace collar to button and buttonhole bands.

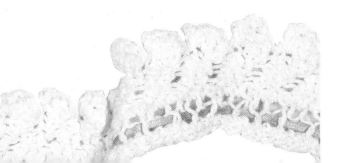

Learn the ropes with cables

Cable patterns are one of the simplest methods of achieving a textured look on knitting. They can be spaced out in panels or worked as an all-over fabric. The patterns given here are just a selection from the scores of possible variations.

Cables add an interesting feature to a garment and are easy to knit. They can be worked in a variety of patterns and sizes ranging from chunky rope-like cables on husky sportswear to intricate braid effects for panels and dainty miniature twists on baby garments.

The stitches which are twisted to form the cables are usually worked in stocking stitch against a reversed stocking stitch or moss stitch background which makes them stand out.

How to work a cable

A cable is formed by a number of stitches changing places with an adjacent number of stitches. The groups of stitches can be moved to the right or to the left or alternately right and left to give different patterns. No more than twelve stitches should be used in a single cable or the fabric will be pulled out of shape. If it is not possible to find a cable needle of the same size as the main needles, use a finer gauge. A cable needle thicker than the main needles will stretch the stitches out of shape.

The abbreviations used for cable patterns are always preceded by full working instructions, either at the beginning of the pattern or the first time a particular cable is used in the pattern. From then on only the abbreviation is given.

As a general guide, the letter C stands for cable. The figure after this represents the *total* number of stitches to be used in a cable twist. This number is divided in half to make the two parts which twist over or under each other. This is followed by the letter B for back or F for front, depending on whether the cable will twist to the right or the left.

The cable needle is held at the front or the back of the work depending on whether the stitch is crossing to the right or the left.

The working methods for simple cables are given below.

Working a cable twist from right to left

For a single cable worked over 6 knit stitches against a purl background, cast on 18 sts.
1st row (Rs) P6, K6, P6.
2nd row K6, P6, K6.
Rep these 2 rows once more.
5th row P6, sl next 3 sts on to a cable needle and hold at the front of the work, ybk to K the next 3 sts from

the left-hand needle, then K3 sts from cable needle – **called C6F**, P6.
6th row As 2nd.
7th row As 1st.
8th row As 2nd.
These 8 rows form the pattern.

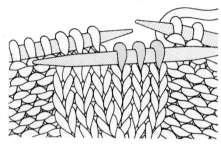

Working a cable twist from left to right

For a single cable worked over 6 knit stitches against a purl background, cast on 18 sts.
1st row (Rs) P6, K6, P6.
2nd row K6, P6, K6.
Rep these 2 rows once more.

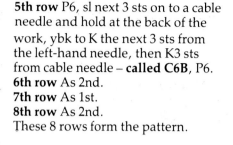

5th row P6, sl next 3 sts on to a cable needle and hold at the back of the work, ybk to K the next 3 sts from the left-hand needle, then K3 sts from cable needle – **called C6B**, P6.
6th row As 2nd.
7th row As 1st.
8th row As 2nd.
These 8 rows form the pattern.

Cast on 100 sts to make this double thickness scarf in DK wool. Work any of the cable patterns on one side of the scarf, and then fold it in half and seam down the side edges.

Alternating cables

Cast on multiples of 12 sts plus 6 sts, eg 30.
1st row (Rs), P6, *K6, P6, rep from * to end.
2nd row K6, *P6, K6, rep from * to end.
Rep 1st and 2nd rows once more.
5th row P6, *C6F, P6, rep from * to end.
6th row As 2nd.
Rep 1st and 2nd rows 3 times more.
13th row P6, *C6B, P6, rep from * to end.
14th row As 2nd.
Rep 1st and 2nd rows once more.
These 16 rows form the pattern.

Honeycomb cables

Cast on multiples of 18 sts plus 6 sts, eg 42.
1st row (Rs), P6, *K12, P6, rep from * to end.
2nd row K6, *P12, K6, rep from * to end.
Rep 1st and 2nd rows once more.
5th row P6, *C6B, C6F, P6, rep from * to end.
6th row As 2nd.
Rep 1st and 2nd rows twice more.
11th row P6, *C6F, C6B, P6, rep from * to end.
12th row As 2nd.
These 12 rows form the pattern.

Braid cables

Double plaited cables

Cast on multiples of 10 sts plus 2 sts, eg 32.

1st row (Rs) P2, *K8, P2, rep from * to end.

2nd row K2, *P8, K2, rep from * to end.

3rd row P2, *(sl next 2 sts on to a cable needle and hold at back of work, ybk and K2 from left-hand needle, then K2 from cable needle – **called C4B**) twice, P2, rep from * to end.

4th row As 2nd.

5th row P2, *K2, sl next 2 sts on to a cable needle and hold at front of work, ybk and K2 from left-hand needle, then K2 from cable needle – **called C4F**, K2, P2, rep from * to end. The 2nd to 5th rows incl form patt.

Cast on multiples of 24 sts plus 6 sts, eg 54.

1st row (Rs) P6, *K18, P6, rep from * to end.

2nd row K6, *P18, K6, rep from * to end.

3rd row P6, *(C6B) 3 times, P6, rep from * to end.

4th row As 2nd.

Rep 1st and 2nd rows once more.

7th row P6, *K3, (C6F) twice, K3, P6, rep from * to end.

8th row As 2nd.

These 8 rows form the pattern.

Index